CW00816287

SELF-CARE PACKAGE

Healing Through The Chakras

SELF-CARE PACKAGE

HEALING THROUGH THE CHAKRAS

Londrelle

ILLUSTRATED BY:
MELISSA KOBY

OFFERINGS

I bow to the breath. I bow to the body. I bow to the senses. I bow to the emotions and feelings. I bow to the heart. I bow to the mind. I bow to the intelligence. I bow to the soul and its loving awareness.
For God. For Guru.
These are my offerings.

CONTENTS

ROOT CHAKRA

SACRAL CHAKRA

INTRODUCTION

Whether you are a beginner on the spiritual path or a spiritual adept, this book serves as a medium to further introduce you to yourself and aid you in your spiritual evolution. There are books and other resources that go deeply into the philosophy of the chakras; this is not one of them. Through the techniques and practices offered in this book, you will gain a deeper insight and understanding of practical ways of healing and working with the seven energy centers, or chakras, in your day-today life. For the beginner and those looking to learn more about the mysteries of the infinite universe within, this book is an offering and a boon to your soul. In it, you will discover methods to improve your physical, mental, and psychological well-being as well as step-by-step practices that will lead you into ever-new awakening, healing, and ascension. If you are on the spiritual path, you will find helpful tools to deepen your practice, as well as your understanding, devotion, and love for the Self within. From your dedicated self-study and consistent practice, the lotus of your soul will blossom.

Your practice is your peace.
The more you practice, the more you
become anchored in peace.

SELF-CARE PACKAGE

KEY TERMS

Asana:

Asana is the third limb in the Eight Limbs of Yoga from Patanjali's *Yoga Sutras*, and it literally means "seat"—specifically the seat you take for meditation. In modern times, the term usually refers to any of the various postures assumed during the practice of yoga.

Bija Mantra:

A Bija mantra (seed mantra) is assigned to each chakra, and each petal of the lotus blossom carries a Sanskrit syllable that is described as the "guardian" of that particular chakra. When we repeat the mantra belonging to a chakra in meditation, we unite our consciousness with the energy and consciousness of the corresponding chakra.

Chakra:

Chakra means "wheel" or "turning." A chakra operates like a powerhouse in the way that it generates and stores energy, with energy from the cosmos pulled in vigorously at these points. The drain of a bathtub can be used to illustrate how the chakras work. When the plug is removed from a bathtub full of water, the water is sucked into the drainpipe, and the rotating water forms a vortex. This is how a chakra functions. In the same way that water is sucked into a drainpipe forming a whirlpool, cosmic energy is drawn into the chakras in a circular motion and guided toward the next point of intersection. This cosmic radiation influences and guides our feelings, thoughts, and nature according to our spiritual and karmic susceptibility.

Hatha yoga:

Hatha yoga is a generic term that refers to any type of yoga that teaches physical postures.

Mudra:

Mudra means "seal," "gesture," or "mark." Yoga mudras are symbolic gestures often practiced with the hands and fingers. They facilitate the flow of energy in the subtle body and enhance one's journey inward.

Prana:

Prana is the creative vibration or energy that activates and sustains life in the body. Prana is also called "life force." This life force is highly concentrated and in its purest form in the breath.

Pranayama:

Conscious control of prana. The yoga science of pranayama is the direct way to consciously disconnect the mind from the life functions and sensory perceptions that tie us to body consciousness. The practice of pranayama thus frees our consciousness from the body consciousness and enables us to commune with the indwelling Spirit. All scientific techniques that bring about the union of soul and Spirit may be classified as yoga, and pranayama is the greatest yogic method for attaining this divine union.

Sadhana:

Sadhana is a Sanskrit word that means "daily spiritual practice." It's the foundation for your personal, individual effort to communicate with the divine inside of you and all around you. It is the main tool you use to work on yourself to achieve your purpose in life.

HOW TO USE
THIS BOOK

Check in with yourself. How is your energy? How do you really feel? Where is your consciousness seated? If these questions seem foreign or unrelatable to you, then this book will help you develop a deeper and profound relationship with yourself so that you may be able to answer these types of questions and know what steps to take to consciously heal and work with your energy. Energy is everything, and everything is energy. The body that you have is a wave of energy. The food that you eat to bring energy and wellness to the body is also energy. Even the words that you are reading are energy and have a vibrational effect on your body, mind, and feelings. Energy is not only what we emit, but energy is what we are and what we are made of. Albert Einstein once said, "Everything is energy and that's all there is to it. Match the frequency of the reality you want, and you cannot help but get that reality." One way to "match frequencies" is to work with the chakras. Chakra work allows us to learn to master our energy and become conscious creators on this plane of existence.

Each chakra carries with it a particular energy and consciousness that helps us navigate through our thoughts, feelings, emotions, and life experiences. When our energy is off, we are out of balance and out of tune with our chakras and the divine energy they emit. By bringing our awareness and attention to any of the seven chakras, we tune in with their pure vibrations and energetically restore balance to our being. It is not absolutely necessary to have all of the chakras open and activated at the same time. We aim for balance and harmony. The seven primary chakras, which are aligned vertically in the spine and in the brain, can be compared to the finger holes on a flute. If a flutist blew into the instrument's mouthpiece without placing any fingers over the holes, the tune would either be flat or nonexistent. It is only when the player blows into the flute while simultaneously opening and closing certain holes that a melody can be heard.

The spine is your flute, and on this flute, you learn to play the melody of your life's song. This requires you to be in tune with yourself and know when certain chakras are blocked, need to be open and activated, or when they are overactive and need to be dialed down. When your instrument is out of tune, it is difficult to play a song, and even more difficult to play in harmony with others. Every practice in this book offers a way for you to tune in with yourself and get in tune with the energy and vibration of each chakra. As you tap into you, you fine-tune the instruments of the body, mind, and soul and begin to live in perfect harmony with yourself and the life around you. Whenever your energy is off, you may return to this book to find the energetic fix you need to realign. To keep your energy from getting out of tune, you may use this book daily to check in with yourself and make adjustments where needed. It is my wish and affirmation that you will grow, ascend, and awaken to Truth that's even beyond my capacity to explain. Thank you for allowing this book to be a portal into the deeper aspects of you. Travel deep and stay free!

Grounding is essential for growth. Root yourself in the present, be here, and let life nourish your evolution.

SELF-CARE CHECK-IN

Sit briefly with the following questions; they will determine if you need to tune in and align with the balanced energy of the root chakra.

- Do you feel stuck, stagnant, or out of place in the world?

- Are you struggling to find peace where you currently are?

- Is your life a mess and lacking organization?

- Have you been procrastinating on a big project lately?

- Are you struggling to get ideas and projects started?

- Have you found yourself being easily distracted or lacking focus?

- Has your patience been running thin?

- Have you been stubborn lately—unwilling to adjust?

- Are you struggling or dissatisfied financially?

- Do you feel connected to others?

- Do you feel connected to you?

- Where are you mentally? And are you there physically?

After checking in with yourself, are you satisfied with the answers you gave to the questions above? Do you see where you need some help? This is where the shift starts to happen, and you begin to consciously understand and master your energy. If your answers to the questions above were unsatisfactory to you, this is an indication to focus on the root chakra today. You can find the Root Chakra Sadhana in the following chapter. The practice should take you no more than an hour, but there are also auxiliary practices and exercises you may do to further balance the energy in the root chakra. If you are working on this center, please try not to mix the practices from other chapters with it. The more focus you place on a particular center, the more that energy awakens, and the stronger it becomes. Allow yourself to focus solely on grounding today. Plant your roots deep and feel the earth's energy becoming your own.

●

When we resist what is now, we repel what is to come. Accept and allow. Everything eventually works itself out.

●

GROUND YOURSELF:
ROOT CHAKRA
OVERVIEW

In any endeavor, whether it be spiritual or material, being grounded is of the highest importance. If we are not grounded, we cannot grow. Think of yourself and your life as a tree. The winds and storms that Nature may bring easily uproot a tree that is not planted and deeply rooted in the soil of the earth. When we are not grounded, we can be easily distracted or drawn away from our goals, purpose, and, most importantly, ourselves. Our minds become fickle, and our emotions, easily swayed by the trials and tests that life may bring. We can also lack a sense of direction, focus, and trust in ourselves, our journey, and the unseen Force or Spirit that guides us. Grounding grants us peace. It plants us in the present moment, in the here and now. And from this blooms the fruit of focus, trust, clarity, and inner guidance. On the spiritual path, grounding reminds us of our dedication to our practice. Our practice is the set of disciplines that lead us into a deeper understanding of ourselves, our lives, and ultimately into Truth and realization. Practice is to your spiritual journey what water is to a seed. Through a consistent and dedicated practice of our sadhana, we invoke the soul to awaken from its slumber and reveal the glory of Spirit.

ALONG MY JOURNEY

In my own spiritual journey, I've found that I have to continually remind myself that "The practice is the goal." Sometimes, I notice that I am seeking immediate results of flexibility and suppleness from my hatha yoga practices or trying to force myself to have specific experiences in meditation. While doing so, I find that I am entirely negligent of the actual practice. And as a result, I notice myself losing attentiveness and interest in the practice itself. When this occurs, I have to remember to ground myself, pause, and bring the mind back to the *essential* goal—the practice.

So, this comes as a reminder or maybe even a forewarning. When you feel slightly disinterested, hopeless, or even frustrated with your spiritual journey, remind yourself that the practice is the goal. Remember to recenter and ground yourself in the purpose of your practice. Remember the disciplines that you are being taught. They may often seem trivial or tedious, but their simplicity and practicality should not be taken lightly. You have sought the way to self-transformation, healing, and understanding, and the practice has come to be your guru. Through practice, you will learn. Through practice, you will grow.

Over the years, I've started my days with the same practice. There are occasions on which I don't feel like stretching, chanting mantras, meditating, or doing breathing exercises. Still, I commit myself to the practice because I realize the value it adds to my life. I know that every time I practice, it is an energetic investment, and the return of this investment may not come immediately, but it does come when I most need it. The peace that I nurture in meditation finds me when I encounter obstacles in business or disagreements with others. The hours I spend on the mat keep me mentally stable and flexible when things don't go as planned. When I least expect it, I often become overwhelmed with great floods of joy, inner knowing, creative insight, clarity, understanding, and divine bliss. I find joy in knowing that every day's practice leads to tomorrow's peace. If I practice today, I will have peace tomorrow. And if I practice tomorrow, I will have peace today.

ABOUT THIS CHAKRA

The Sanskrit name for the root chakra is Muladhara. Mula means "root" and adhara means "base" or "support." The root or Muladhara chakra is located at the base of the spine. It is the foundation of our connection with the material world and the point from which we grow upward on the spiritual journey. The Muladhara chakra is associated with the color red and the element of earth. It is symbolized by a lotus flower with four petals and is responsible for our sense of smell. The theme of this chakra is safety, security, survival, stability, and grounding.

When this chakra is active and open, we develop a more peaceful and trusting Nature. Peace allows us to be present, to be aware of our thoughts and emotions, and how they are shaping our everyday experience. Peace also grants us clarity, and from this clarity comes trust, the trust needed to feel safe and secure in our bodies and our environment. The spiritual aspirant who has mastered this center's energy builds a strong foundation upon which spiritual and material growth will be erected. The Muladhara chakra is also known as the "money center." It has a strong influence on our material accomplishments and our ability to attract wealth, prosperity, success, and worldly power.

Though it may often be seen as taboo in the realm of spirituality, money is needed for our basic needs, survival, health, and service in the world.

Further developing the root chakra allows us to have a healthy relationship with money and is the key to a life of material abundance. Money or currency, in the physical sense, reflects the inner wealth and power that we possess. It represents our ability and capacity to call upon and manifest the things necessary to sustain our lives. Our relationship with money and our need for it determines how much we can call forth. When greed enters our lives, then money becomes the root of all sorts of evil. The root or Muladhara chakra becomes overactive, imbalanced, and can sometimes be blocked when our needs are overtaken by our greed. Those who go about opening this center with wisdom gain the steadiness of mind and discipline needed to handle the material benefits that come with the awakening of this sacred energy center. They use wealth not only for their own gain but for the growth of the world as well. To them, wealth is happiness, and happiness is to be shared.

The energy in the Muladhara chakra challenges us to be disciplined, grounded, and dedicated to our chosen paths, goals, and deepest desires. Dedication means loyalty. Loyalty is the foundation of inward growth and self-evolution. As no structure can adequately be built without a stable foundation, all upward progress on the spiritual path is dependent on the energy that flows through this center. When working on your root chakra, always be intentional and centered in your practice. Do not allow yourself to be distracted or mentally taken away from the time you have dedicated to concentrating on this center. Any lack of attentiveness will result in an unstable foundation. This results in an unsteady progression toward building a life of peace, abundance, trust, and spiritual evolution. The dedication and effort you put into grounding yourself will be the nourishment you need to grow yourself.

SIGNS OF BALANCE AND IMBALANCE

When your root chakra is open or balanced, you may experience or feel the following:

Trust in your life and journey	Flexibility (physical and mental)	Financial stability
A sense of peace and ease	Less worry and anxiety	Patience
A sense of safety and security	Released attachments	Fearlessness
		Organized
		Grounded

When your root chakra is blocked or imbalanced, you may experience or feel the following:

Fear	Impatience	Stubbornness
Inertia	Unorganized	Mental instability
Greed	Insecurity	Financial instability
Anxiety	Lack of trust	Inertia or sluggishness
Worry	Inflexibility	

Physical signs and symptoms of imbalances in the root chakra may also include:

Lower back pain	Nasal congestion	Inflammation
Problems in the colon	Bladder issues	Cramps
	Lack of energy	

ROOT CHAKRA SADHANA

AFFIRMATION

"When I ground myself, I grow myself.
From the earth, I grow. From the earth, I bloom."

MEDITATION

Listen to the "Ground Yourself: Root Chakra Meditation."
Available on streaming apps and YouTube.

EXERCISE

What are some things you admire about the earth? Write them
down or spend a few moments vocalizing these things. Feel
that these qualities are also manifested within you, and practice
expressing these virtues today.

POSE OF THE DAY

MALASANA (GARLAND POSE)

Malasana or garland pose supports and balances the root chakra, making it the perfect asana for grounding ourselves. It also helps calm the mind and brings an overall sense of relaxation to the body and mind. We can store a tremendous amount of negative energy in the center of our lower body, and this energy can show up in our lives as physical pain or discomfort. Malasana works with the downward flowing apana vayu current, which helps us release tension and toxicity from our bodies.

GROUND YOURSELF:ROOT CHAKRA

BENEFITS

Opens hips and eases lower back pain	Improves digestion Improves posture	Strengthens knees and legs Opens chest and shoulders

HOW TO DO MALASANA (GARLAND POSE)

1. Come to a standing position with your legs shoulder width apart or slightly wider. (Deeply inhale to the count of six as you prepare to squat.)

2. Bend the knees and lower your butt toward the floor to come into a squatting position. (Exhale the breath as you gradually lower yourself down into the squat.)

3. If your toes want to point out slightly on either side, it's okay. Eventually, you're working toward keeping the feet closer to parallel.

4. Bring your arms inside your knees and bend the elbows to bring the palms together into the prayer position.

5. With your hands at your heart center, use your elbows to gently press up against your knees as you stretch your groin and open your hips.

6. Be sure to keep your spine straight, your butt moving toward the floor, and your shoulders relaxed away from your ears.

7. Stay here for six breaths, then straighten the legs to come out. (To get out of the pose, you may also sit back onto your butt.)

8. Try repeating this three to six times to get the full benefits of this pose. Feel free to flow into any other asanas that complement today's practice listed in the next section.

Asanas that balance the root chakra:

Corpse Pose
(Savasana)

Full Body Stretch
Pose (Supta Utthita
Tadasana)

Easy Pose
(Sukhasana)

Knees to Chest
Pose (Apanasana)

Bridge Pose
(Setu Bandha
Sarvangasana)

Head-to-Knee Pose
(Janu Sirsasana)

Wide Child Pose
(Utthita Balasana)

Garland Pose
(Malasana)

Dangling Pose
(Baddha Hasta
Uttanasana)

Chair Pose
(Utkatasana)

Revolved Chair
Pose (Parivrtta
Utkatasana)

Wide-Legged
Forward Fold
(Prasarita
Padottanasana)

Warrior II
(Virabhadrasana II)

Mountain Pose
(Tadasana)

Crescent Lunge
Pose (Anjaneyasana)

Tree Pose
(Vrksansana)

●

Whenever you're feeling uprooted or out of place, give yourself permission to come back home. You are home— come back to you.

●

REMINDER

Those who are not grounded cannot grow. Release the desire to be anywhere other than where you are now. Life wants to nourish and flourish you here. Plant yourself in the present, and let life grow you. Often, the biggest challenge we face is our unwillingness to trust the process. We want to reap the harvest of success, healing, and ascension before we've tilled and cultivated the land of our hearts and minds. It's important to note that the spiritual journey is not about becoming anything—you are already that. It is a gradual process of unbecoming—cleansing, purifying, detoxing, and decluttering so that the real you can shine through. With every practice, allow yourself to become a bit less burdened, a bit less worried, a bit less bound by this world, and a bit more grounded in the boundlessness of your soul's nature.

Despite life's difficulties and challenges, remember who you are and keep reminding yourself of your fullness. You are enough, as you are—and everything that is present is here to remind you of all that you are. It may be uncomfortable. It may even be painful, but let nothing disturb you, deplete you, or deter you from living in your fullness. Be rooted in your being and your ever connectedness with Spirit. There is neither distance nor separation between you and your Creator. The two are really one. As you become more grounded in this realization, you will find the hidden hands of grace gently guiding you and leading you to the accomplishment of all that you seek. Stay grounded in God, and you will grow exponentially in life.

ROOT CHAKRA
AUXILIARY PRACTICES

In this section, you will find additional exercises, tips, and readings that can be implemented in today's routine. The exercises can be done in any order, at any point in time during the day. To stay in alignment with the work within this theme, it is best to practice these exercises on the days that you have chosen to focus on your root chakra. However, it is okay to practice any of these exercises whenever you feel inclined to do so.

ROOT CHAKRA MANTRA: LAM

The Bija or seed mantra for the root chakra is LAM. If you feel sluggish, uprooted, distracted, or disconnected from the earth and the physical realm, chanting this mantra will help activate the root chakra and restore balance.

HOW TO PRACTICE

1. In a seated or standing position, focus your mind's attention on the root chakra (in the base of the spine). Close your eyes, feel, and visualize a vibrant red light glowing at this center.

2. Inhale to the count of six, and as you do so, imagine that the red sphere of light is increasing in size.

3. Hold your breath until the count of three. While you do so, maintain the feeling and visualization of the red ball of light radiating at the base of your spine.

4. Exhale, and as you do so, chant LAM (LUM as in alum). Visualize the light becoming smaller and finally being absorbed into this energy center. With your attention still focused on the base of your spine, rest here for twelve seconds and repeat this exercise two more times.

5. If the breathing counts are too long or short for you, feel free to adjust them to accommodate your lung capacity. Do not hold your breath for extreme periods of time, as you may cause damage to your lungs, heart, or brain. As a rule of thumb, the length of time you hold your breath can be twice, or half, the length of your inhale.

TIP: If you inhale to the count of six, hold the breath for a three count. Or if you inhale to the count of six, hold the breath to the count of twelve. I do not recommend holding the breath for more than thirty seconds. Be smart! Be safe!

ROOT CHAKRA MUDRA

GYAN MUDRA

Gyan Mudra is often considered one of the most important mudras. It has been practiced for thousands of years by yogis of various paths. It is known as the "mudra of knowledge," as it summons the light and guidance of our highest selves and prepares the mind to receive its wisdom. This mudra also lifts us to a state of calmness, allowing us to flow with ease through daily difficulties and life lessons.

HOW TO PRACTICE

While sitting in a comfortable position, gently bring the tips of your thumb and index finger to touch. Keep your other three fingers together but relax and place them on your thighs or knees. Do this with both your left and right hand as you practice the following pranayama exercise.

GROUND YOURSELF:ROOT CHAKRA

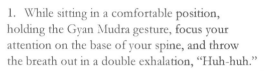

ROOT CHAKRA PRANAYAMA EXERCISE

1. While sitting in a comfortable position, holding the Gyan Mudra gesture, focus your attention on the base of your spine, and throw the breath out in a double exhalation, "Huh-huh."

2. Inhale completely and fill the root chakra with prana.

3. Without holding the breath, exhale completely and allow this energy to flow out of the root chakra.

4. As you come to the end of the exhale, mentally or verbally say, "I AM."

5. Allow a brief pause, inhale, and repeat this exercise for four minutes.

TIP: After the first rep, you do not need to perform the double exhalation in step one. Continue on to steps two through five.

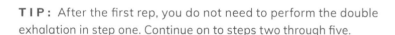

Every breath is an invitation into you. Into love, into peace, into joy, into Truth

ROOT CHAKRA CRYSTALS

The following is a list of crystals you may use to help stimulate the root chakra. These crystals may be worn as jewelry, kept in your purse, pocket, or placed on your desk or yoga mat during practice. You can even place them in your bathtub as you soak and take a nice relaxing bath. There are no hard rules about when and how you can use crystals; just have fun including them in your practice.

Red Jasper

Alleviates stress, increases focus, and helps establish new spiritual disciplines; enhances creativity, strength, and stamina; and promotes peace, balance, and emotional stability

Black Tourmaline

Helps protect and purify energy, cleanses the emotional body, increases physical vitality, reduces stress, clears the aura, dissolves fear, and removes blockages

Poppy Jasper

Brings courage, strength, and willpower—inspires new ideas—and promotes vitality, enthusiasm, and mental fortitude

Bloodstone

Promotes mental clarity, courage, confidence, and discernment

Smokey Quartz

Helps overcome stress, fear, jealousy, anger, and depression; enhances mood and improves survival instincts; aids in concentration and helps improve communication difficulties

Red Carnelian

Helps you make better decisions, assists in taking action toward goals, inspires ambition, confidence, and stimulates willpower

Hematite:

Helps with pain relief, improves memory, balances energy, and clears confusion; promotes calmness, tranquility, and grounding

Garnet:

Removes energy blockages, clears bad karma, and offers energetic protection for travelers; helps you feel grounded, safe, and secure

ROOT CHAKRA AROMATHERAPY

Below, you will find a list of essential oils that can be used to stimulate and balance the root chakra.

Cypress	Juniper	Sandalwood
Geranium	Mandarin	Spearmint
Ginger	Petitgrain	Ylang-ylang

ROOT CHAKRA JUICE

"EARTH'S EMBRACE"

Designed to open and stimulate the root chakra, this earth-rich juice is sure to help you feel grounded, supported, and balanced while also bringing an energetic increase to the body and mind. Refreshing and restoring, *Earth's Embrace* brings into manifestation feelings of gratitude, grounding, revitalization, focus, and pure joy!

Ingredients

2 red apples
1 cup diced pineapples
1 carrot

2 beets
2 inches ginger root

DIRECTIONS

1. Working in this order, process the apple, pineapple, carrot, beet (peeled), and finally the ginger through a juicer according to the manufacturer's directions. (No juicer? See Tip.)

2. Fill 16-oz. glass with ice, if desired, and pour the juice into the glass.

TIP: If you don't have a juicer, cut and place these ingredients in your blender and add 8–14 oz. of water. After blending, over a large bowl, pour the contents into a nut-milk bag. Squeeze the bag until all the liquid has been removed from the bag and only the fiber remains. Discard the fiber and carefully pour the juice from the bowl into a glass or mason jar.

Drink on an empty stomach to get the most health benefits.

BENEFITS

Heals acne	Reduces puffy eyes	Detoxifies blood
Anticancer	Improves liver function	Supports eye health
Antibacterial	Improves brain function	Lowers blood pressure
Prevents dementia	Anti-inflammatory	Improves energy levels
Improves digestion		

ROOT CHAKRA FOODS

The following is a list of foods that help stimulate the root chakra. Feel free to include them in your diet on the days in which you focus on this center.

ROOT VEGETABLES: Potatoes, sweet potatoes, parsnips, onions, carrots, beets, rutabagas, turmeric, kohlrabi, radish, rhubarb, horseradish

FRUITS: Apples, strawberries, raspberries, pomegranate, cherries, watermelon, tomatoes, guava, cranberries, red pear

HERBS: Chive, paprika, cinnamon, cayenne, rosemary, elderberry, sage, carob

PROTEINS: Quinoa, oats, beans, mushrooms, peanut butter, almond butter

TEA: Hibiscus, Valerian, Goji berry, pink peppercorns

ROOT CHAKRA AFFIRMATIONS

I am grounding my energies in the present moment.

I know that there is nowhere to be but here.

As long as I am here, I am exactly where I need to be.

I am grounding my mind in the now.

As long as I am present, I am exactly where I need to be.

I am grounding my spirit in the eternal now.

All that exists is now. I will be here. I will be now.

I am exactly where I need to be.

I am not alone in my journey.

I trust that I am divinely guided and protected.

I feel secure in my body.

I feel safe in my surroundings.

The earth is my home.

The earth is my body.

I take care of the earth.

I take care of my body.

I am deeply grounded and planted in the soil of Mother Earth.

I am nurtured. I am cared for. I am loved.

The roots of my life connect me with all life.

The whole world is my family.

I am supported everywhere that I go.

The whole universe is my tribe.

I am supported in everything that I do.

I trust my path.

I trust my journey.

I trust my soul.

I am completely here and at peace.

I am completely now and at peace.

I am completely present and at peace.

My mind is free and calm.

My body is free and calm.

My soul is free and calm.

I am free and calm.

I am free.

POINTS OF DAILY INTROSPECTION

At the start of each day, the spiritual aspirant makes it a habit to practice impartial introspection. While viewing themselves with the soul's love and wisdom, inquire as to things that limit and suppress the expression of their highest nature. The following is a short list of introspective prompts that you may reflect upon during your morning meditation or journaling sessions.

- What bad habits am I hoarding, and what can I do today to free myself from these binding mental tendencies?

- On a scale from one to ten, ten being the most efficient, how disciplined have I been lately? Am I satisfied with this? If not, what can I do to ensure that I improve this?

- On a scale from one to ten, ten being the most efficient, how focused have I been lately? Am I satisfied with this? If not, what can I do to improve?

- What is the one thing I will do today that cannot be put off until tomorrow?

- What one word will keep me grounded and be my mantra today?

POINTS OF NIGHTLY INTROSPECTION

At the end of each day, the spiritual aspirant makes it a habit to impartially introspect on that day's activities. Nightly introspection allows one to see whether they made spiritual progress and remained committed to the tasks, goals, and intentions established at the start of the day. Writing these things in a spiritual diary allows us to clearly see our repetitive faults and our virtues and make adjustments wherever needed. The following is a short list of introspective prompts that you may reflect upon during or after your nightly meditation.

- What was my state of mind today, calm or restless?

- What things, if any, did I allow to "uproot" me?

- What lessons did I learn from these things?

- What good habits did I reinforce today?

- Am I satisfied with my total effort toground myself today?

GROUNDING YOURSELF CAN ALSO LOOK LIKE:

- Spending time in nature
- Listening to feel-good music
- Walking in the grass barefoot
- Taking time to rest your body
- Spending time in solitude
- Doing yoga or going to the gym
- Reading your favorite children's book
- Coloring or drawing
- Stargazing, sun gazing, or moon gazing
- Cuddling with your partner

or pet

- Breathing consciously
- Hugging or touching a tree
- Sunbathing
- Stretching
- Going for a run or walk
- Touching soil, rock, or grass
- Doing color therapy
- Nature gazing

Let yourself feel.

That's how you self-heal.

SELF-CARE CHECK-IN

Sit briefly with the following questions; they will determine if you need to tune in and align with the balanced energy of the sacral chakra.

- Do you feel emotionally withdrawn or disconnected?

- Do you feel creatively uninspired or blocked?

- Are you, or on the brink of, feeling depressed?

- Have you been moody?

- Are your hips stiff?

- Do you dance or play often?

- Do you feel an urge to express yourself emotionally?

- Have you been avoiding drinking water lately?

- Are you experiencing the resurfacing of trauma?

- Are you healing from something emotionally?

- Do you feel unwanted or undesired?

- Is pleasure absent from your life?

- Are you feeling guilty or ashamed about something?

After checking in with yourself, are you satisfied with the answers you gave to the questions above? Do you see where you need some help? This is where the shift starts to happen, and you begin to consciously understand and master your energy. If your answers to the questions above were unsatisfactory to you, this is an indication to focus on the sacral chakra today. You can find the Sacral Chakra Sadhana in the following chapter. The practice should take you no more than an hour, but you may also do auxiliary practices and exercises to further balance the energy in the sacral center. If you are working on this chakra, please try not to mix the practices from other chapters with it. The more focus you place on a particular center, the more that energy awakens, and the stronger it becomes. Allow yourself to focus solely on embracing yourself today. Tune in with your emotions. Feel, dance, create, play, flow.

Embrace all parts of you. Accept that this version of you is also worthy of the fullness of life.

EMBRACE YOURSELF:
SACRAL CHAKRA
SADHANA OVERVIEW

When we are out of touch with our emotions, we have disconnected from an important part of ourselves. Whether they are seen as good or bad, emotions help us navigate through life more efficiently. They act as a warning system and let us know where our thoughts and consciousness are centered. If we ignore our emotions, we can end up digressing through life recklessly—harming and hurting everyone we come into contact with. In the male-dominant society we currently live in, we are often urged to be less sensitive. We are told to hide or even suppress our deepest feelings and emotions and that we have to be tough to make it in this world. As a result, we have suppressed our feminine nature and thus have created an imbalance both within ourselves and in the society in which we operate. If we persist in our disregard for emotional health and well-being, we can become rigid, unsympathetic, and often emotionally numb. Emotional suppression can lead to depression, and in some cases, melancholia.

Contrary to popular opinion, it is okay to feel angry, it's okay to feel sad, and it's okay to feel hurt. The feelings are there to be felt. If we can't feel it, we won't heal it. Obviously, being angry, sad, or hurt are not positive and progressive emotional states that we should persist in, but that doesn't mean we shouldn't embrace or allow ourselves to express them. When we learn to accept and embrace our emotions, we can allow them to flow through us in a healthy way. Embracing our emotions allows us to make way for the release. Physical and mental health is vital to vibrant and high vibrational living, but let us not forget about our emotions—they matter too. When we embrace ourselves, we must strive to do so in fullness and not in parts. Embrace all parts of you, accept that this version of you is also worthy of the fullness of life.

ALONG MY JOURNEY

The wounds of our past are, in some way, still present. They show up in our thinking habits, our unconscious actions, and emotional reactions. Though they may not be physically present or noticeable, these wounds burden our spirits in the most daunting ways. I'm not exempt; I, too, have wounds—deep ones at that. My wounds are the product of childhood trauma. I was raised by a single mother, who was only seventeen when she gave birth to me, and to add, she had to deal with my father's death before my first birthday. As a child herself, I'm sure she didn't have the resources and support to cope mentally or emotionally with all that burdened her at the time.

From a very young age, I was always told that I had to be tougher than I was. Tougher usually meant less emotional. Being an empathetic and sensitive child, I would often be threatened, teased, and sometimes physically abused because I was, in my mother's eyes, "soft." In my home, I wasn't allowed to cry or provided a safe space to express myself emotionally. Thus, I grew to be very reserved, introverted, and for the most part, emotionally detached. Even as I write these words, I am revisited by the memories of my emotional hurt and trauma. The emotional suppression and abuse I experienced throughout my adolescent years resulted in me being less sensitive to others and unwilling to emotionally open up to others.

As I become more aware of how my childhood has affected my relationship with myself and others, I'm compelled to go back into the darkness of my youth and compassionately offer myself light and love. Working through the shadows by sitting with the pain and allowing myself to relive the things I experienced as a child has been my method of self-healing. Sometimes the pain is unbearable, other days, I can tolerate it, but the more I sit with it and give myself permission to feel, the more I heal. I've stopped running away from the shadows. I've learned to face them. I've learned to embrace me—all of me.

ABOUT THIS CHAKRA

The Sanskrit name of the sacral chakra is Swadhisthana. Swa means "self" or "prana" and adhisthana means "dwelling place." The literal translation of Swadhisthana is "The dwelling place of the self." The sacral or Swadhisthana chakra is located in the spine, directly behind the genitals. It is associated with the color orange and is responsible for our sense of taste. This center is symbolized by a lotus flower with six petals and is ruled by the water element. Our emotions, much like water, can be deep, calm, shallow, or restless. The energy in the sacral chakra calls for us to be in tune with the depth and flow of our emotions, feeling them with a willingness to understand how they shape and affect our lives. When emotions flow in a healthy way, they bring joy, pleasure, and fulfillment and allow us to feel connected with all aspects of life. When the flow of our emotions is blocked or left unchecked, it can lead to a chaotic, volatile, or even lifeless existence. Relationships, feelings, emotions, sexuality, play, and creativity are all associated with the energy that flows through this chakra. The six lotus petals of  the sacral chakra symbolically represent the six obstacles on the path of spiritual development. Those obstacles are lust, anger, greed, pride, delusional emotional attachment, and envy.

When the sacral chakra's energy flows outward and downward, it manifests as passion, material desire, movement, creativity on the physical plane, and the expression or desire for sensual pleasure. When this energy is flowing inward and upward, it manifests as inner joy, self-satisfaction, fulfillment, and creative inspiration on the spiritual plane. Whether it be on the material or spiritual plane, all pleasure is a sacred and essential aspect of this experience. Physical pleasure brings gratification and satisfaction on the plane of the senses. It allows us to enjoy and appreciate the beauty of the material world. Spiritual pleasure brings bliss and supreme fulfillment. It lifts our consciousness and brings us back to Source—back to God. Life is a divine play, a dance between Spirit and Nature. When this center is balanced, we feel a deep interconnectedness between ourselves and the world around us.

After the Muladhara, the Swadhisthana chakra is the center that demands much of our attention and time. Upon fulfilling our basic needs for survival, stability, and money, the consciousness then begins to seek out pleasure, enjoyment, and the development of relationships. Relationships act as a mirror and provide us with an opportunity to see and reform ourselves. They help reveal the qualities that we may lack or need to improve upon. They also provide the necessary support and encouragement we often so desperately need to progress emotionally, mentally, materially, and spiritually.

The sacral chakra calls for us to develop and maintain healthy relationships, not just with others but also with ourselves. The type of relationship that we have with ourselves will always reflect in the types of relationships we attract in our lives. Relationships have been given to us so that we may better understand our emotions and learn how to heal ourselves through their power. When we embrace and work to understand our emotions, we can heal our relationships, past traumas, and release any emotional baggage that may be a burden to us. Healing the emotional body is the gateway into profound understanding, freedom, and self-transformation.

As you activate and balance this sacred place, be willing to sit with and embrace all the hurt and inner turmoil that may resurface in the process. The feelings are there to be felt. The hurt is there to be *healed*. Embrace yourself lovingly and see yourself through the eyes of the Divine.

SIGNS OF BALANCE AND IMBALANCE

When your sacral chakra is open or balanced, you may experience or feel the following:

Playful
Nurturing
Emotionally stable
Emotionally expressive

Socially connected
Sensually connected
Imaginative and creative
Ability to adapt to change

Healthy relationships
The ability to self-nurture
Definiteness of desire (you know what you want)

When your sacral chakra is blocked or imbalanced, you may experience or feel the following:

Depression
Fear of change
Lack of creative ambition
Emotionally detached
Lack of self-worth

Frequent mood swings
Lack of vulnerability
Sensually addicted
Feelings of guilt and shame

Inability to express emotions
Inability to nurture yourself
Dysfunctional relationships
Weak or unhealthy boundaries

Physical signs and symptoms of imbalances in the sacral chakra may also include:

Anemia
Low energy
Infertility
Low libido
Hormonal imbalances

Hip pain or discomfort
Joint stiffness or discomfort
Kidney issues

Menstrual issues
Lack of flexibility
Lower back pain

SACRAL CHAKRA SADHANA

AFFIRMATION

"The fullness of life flows through me—I am enough."

MEDITATION

Listen to the "Embrace Yourself: Sacral Chakra Meditation."
Available on streaming apps and YouTube.

EXERCISE

Write a short letter to a younger version of yourself.

Offer them words of healing, love, and guidance. Let them know where you are now and how much you have grown.

POSE OF THE DAY

ARDHA KAPOTASANA
(HALF PIGEON POSE)

As you may know, our bodies are affected by our emotions as well. When we experience any type of emotional abuse, suppression, or trauma, we have a natural tendency to tense certain muscles and parts of our bodies. Through repetitive tension and traumatic experiences, energy from our emotions can be "trapped" in the hips, glutes, and other muscles in the sacral region. Ardha Kapotasana or half pigeon pose is the perfect pose to open up those hips and release the energy of trapped emotions. This pose also teaches us to sit with discomfort so that we may open ourselves up to the deep understanding that our emotions bring.

BENEFITS

Opens hips	Strengthens lower back	Opens the chest and improves breathing
Improves mood	Improves spine flexibility	

HOW TO DO ARDHA KAPOTASANA (HALF PIGEON POSE)

1. From the downward-facing dog position, inhale, and carefully bring your left foot toward your left wrist, then place your knee on the mat.

2. Straighten your right leg, and stretch it toward the back of your mat. Your legs will resemble the shape of the number 7.

3. If your shins are not parallel with the top of your mat, it's okay. Rest the left ankle down in a position that is most comfortable for you.

4. Make sure your shoulders and core are stacked over your hips.

5. Exhale and walk your hands forward and gently lower your forehead to the mat. (If this is difficult, please feel free to stack your forearms and rest your forehead on your arms.)

6. After a few deep breaths, walk your hands back up and straighten your arms. Step the left leg back into the downward-facing dog position and switch sides.

7. Try repeating this three to six times to get the full benefits of this pose. Feel free to flow into any other asanas that complement today's practice.

Asanas that balance the sacral chakra:

Reclined Bound Angle Pose (Supta Baddha Konasana)

Bound angle pose (Baddha Konasana)

Frog Pose (Mandukasana)

Cobra Pose (Bhujangasana)

Bow Pose (Dhanurasana)

Pigeon Pose (Eka Pada Rajakapotasana)

Seated Forward Bend (Paschimottanasana)

Cross-Legged Twist Pose (Parivrtta Sukhasana)

Half Lord Of The Fishes - Ardha Matsyendrasana

Camel Pose (Ustrasana)

Low Lunge (Anjaneyasana)

Triangle Pose – Trikonasana

Wide Legged Forward Bend C (Prasarita Padottanasana C)

Reverse Warrior Pose (Viparita Virabhadrasana)

Goddess Pose (Utkata Konasana

REMINDER

How we feel is how we live. Our thoughts and actions are backed by feeling. When we feel good, we do good, we treat others good, and we attract good. When our emotions are low, our vibe is off. When this is the case, we tend to lack the will to do anything or be anything, and we also treat others poorly. Set the intention and make a commitment to check in with your emotions periodically throughout the day. Ask yourself, "How am I feeling?" "How do I want to feel?" and "What is stopping me from feeling the way I want to feel?" We can often get so caught up in our thoughts, goals, and daily routines that we allow our emotions to go unnoticed and unattended. Instead of acknowledging and consciously releasing low vibrational emotions, we end up carrying the burden of these toxic vibrations with us throughout each day. I encourage you to take a few moments every few hours to check in with yourself and emotionally unpack.

Just as you have the ability to speak things into existence, you possess the power to speak them out of existence. While scanning your emotions, if you should find any stagnant or toxic emotions, immediately affirm their release. Cast away these low vibrations and accept your right to live life *vibrantly*. If you want to explore your feelings and emotions, feel free to do so as well. As you explore and listen to them, you grow to learn different ways of coping with and overcoming those emotions that do not fuel or inspire your existence. Embrace your emotions without feeling bad for your current or fluctuating moods. Life is indeed a roller coaster. You won't always be riding high, and you most certainly won't always feel low. Allow yourself to go through the motions. Allow yourself to feel the emotions. All emotions are healthy. It's only when we cling to the thoughts and feelings that emotions inspire that we fail to remain in our true state of bliss. Understanding your emotions is integral to understanding you. All parts of you deserve your attention, compassion, and openness. When you embrace yourself in fullness, that is how you will show up in the world. Just don't stay there and make it your home.

SACRAL CHAKRA AUXILIARY PRACTICES

In this section, you will find additional exercises, tips, and readings that can be implemented in today's routine. The exercises can be done in any particular order, at any point in time during the day. To stay in alignment with the work within this theme, it is best to practice these exercises on the days that you have chosen to focus on your root chakra. However, it is okay to practice any of these exercises whenever you feel inclined to do so.

SACRAL CHAKRA MANTRA: VAM

The Bija, or seed mantra, for the sacral chakra is VAM. If you feel emotionally drained, stressed, or tense, chanting this mantra will help stimulate the sacral center. It is also great to practice before or while undertaking any creative endeavor.

HOW TO PRACTICE

1. In a seated or standing position, focus your mind's attention on the location of the sacral chakra. (In the spine, about the width of two fingers below the waist.) Close your eyes and visualize a vibrant orange light glowing at this center.

2. Inhale to the count of six, and as you do so, imagine that the orange sphere of light is increasing in size.

3. Hold your breath until the count of three. While you do so, maintain the visualization of the orange ball of light radiating in the sacral region.

4. Exhale, and as you do so, chant VAM (VUM as in thumb). Visualize the light becoming smaller and finally being absorbed into this energy center. With your attention still focused on the root chakra, rest here for twelve seconds and repeat this exercise two more times.

5. If the breathing counts are too long or short for you, feel free to adjust them to accommodate your lung capacity. Do not hold your breath for extreme periods of time, as you may cause damage to your lungs, heart, or brain. As a rule of thumb, the length of time you hold your breath can be twice, or half, the length of your inhale.

TIP: If you inhale to the count of six, hold the breath for a three count.Or if you inhale to the count of six, hold the breath to the count of twelve. I do not recommend holding the breath for more than thirty seconds. Be smart! Be safe!

SACRAL CHAKRA MUDRA

Dhyana Mudra is a mudra that can be used to balance the water element in our bodies and stimulate the sacral chakra. Water is associated with emotions and feelings, and this is a mudra that will allow you to bring tranquility, fluidity, and calmness to the emotional body. It is also beneficial in removing any emotional or creative blockages.

HOW TO PRACTICE

Bring yourself to a comfortable seated position. Ensure that your spine is straight and your chin is parallel to the floor. Rest your left hand on your lap, palm facing upward. Now, place your right hand, also with the palms facing upward, inside the left. Touch the tips of your thumbs together, making a circle with your hands. Hold the mudra while practicing the following pranayama exercise.

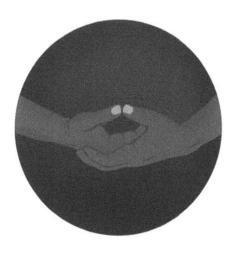

SACRAL CHAKRA PRANAYAMA EXERCISE

While sitting in a comfortable position, focus your mind's attention on the location of the sacral chakra. (In the spine, about the width of two fingers below the waist.) Throw the breath out in a double exhalation, "Huh-huh."

1. Inhale completely and fill the sacral chakra with prana.

2. Without holding the breath, exhale completely and allow this energy to flow from the sacral center back down to the base of your spine.

3. As you come to the end of the exhale, mentally or verbally say, , "As I feel, I heal."

4. Allow a brief pause, inhale and repeat this exercise for six minutes.

Let every breath fill you up, and reaffirm that you are enough.

SACRAL CHAKRA CRYSTALS

The following is a list of crystals you may use to help stimulate the sacral chakra. These crystals may be worn as jewelry, kept in your purse or pocket, or placed on your desk or yoga mat during practice. You can even place them in your bathtub as you soak and take a nice relaxing bath. There are no hard rules as to when and how you can use crystals; just have fun including them in your practice.

Carnelian:

Restores lost vitality and motivation; stimulates creativity; increases fertility; improves concentration; encourages acceptance; promotes positive choices; helps heal lower back problems and arthritis; accelerates healing in bones and ligaments

Orange Calcite:

Reduces fatigue; heals the reproductive system; restores mental and emotional equilibrium; stimulates joy, creativity, and sexuality

Tiger's Eye:

Helps heal depression, anxiety, and bipolar disorder; boosts self-confidence; helps bring ideas into reality; offers vitality; stimulates spiritual growth, kundalini energy, and creativity

Amber:

Brings restoration to the body; eases stomach pains and cramps; heals asthma; increases metabolism; balances emotions; helps release negative energy; removes spiritual obstacles

Orange Moonstone:

Balances emotions; relieves stress, anxiety, and depression; improves mood; promotes fertility; sharpens sensibility; heals the womb; boosts self-image; heals sexual dysfunction; promotes selflessness, honesty, hope, and emotional healing

Sunstone:

Heals depression; increases vitality; heals organs; treats stomach pains and illnesses; assists in self-nurturing; clears all chakras; helps reveal inner talents; enhances intuition; stimulates health, emotional openness, optimism, willpower, and self-healing powers

Goldstone:

Detoxifies the body; strengthens bones; eases arthritis; helps in attaining goals; promotes abundance; alleviates fear; stimulates creativity, sensuality, optimism, willpower, and vitality

Tangerine Quartz

Awakens the inner child; promotes emotional healing; induces joy; helps manifest abundance; removes obstacles; activates creativity and imagination

SACRAL CHAKRA AROMATHERAPY

Below, you will find a list of essential oils that can be used to stimulate and balance the sacral chakra.

Sandalwood	Tangerine	Rosemary
Neroli	Geranium	Jasmine
Orange	Rose	

SACRAL CHAKRA JUICE

"SACRAL SENSATION"

Designed to stimulate and activate the sacral chakra, this juice is guaranteed to get your energy in motion and help bring fresh new life and vibrance into the body. If you're feeling stiff or stagnant, or your creativity is stuck, *Sacral Sensation* will incite movement, flexibility, creativity, inner joy, and a sense of play.

Ingredients

2 mangos
1 orange
1 inch of ginger

3 carrots
⅓ tsp turmeric
A pinch of black pepper

Directions

1. Working in this order, process the mango, orange, ginger, and finally the carrot through a juicer according to the manufacturer's directions. (No juicer? See Tip.)

2. Add to juice 1/3 teaspoon of turmeric and a pinch of black pepper and stir for 15 seconds.

3. Fill 16-oz. glass with ice, if desired, and pour the juice into the glass.

TIP: If you don't have a juicer, cut the ingredients into smaller pieces, place them in your blender, and add 6–8 oz. of alkaline water. After blending, over a large bowl, pour the contents into a nut-milk bag. Squeeze the bag until all the liquid has been removed from the bag and only the fiber remains. Discard the fiber and carefully pour the juice from the bowl into a glass or mason jar.

Drink on an empty stomach to get the most benefits.

BENEFITS

Improves focus
Increases energy
Soothes emotions
Enhances mood
Prevents cancer

Boosts immune system
Increases stamina
Improves memory
Anti-inflammatory

Fights heart disease
Improves skin and sight
Supports kidney health

SACRAL CHAKRA FOODS

The following is a list of foods that help stimulate the sacral chakra. Feel free to include them in your diet on the days in which you focus on this center.

VEGETABLES: Carrots, turmeric, sweet potatoes, pumpkin, acorn squash, butternut squash, orange tomatoes

FRUITS: Oranges, cantaloupe, peaches, apricots, tangerines, mangoes, nectarines

HERBS: Gardenia, coriander, fennel, licorice, sweet paprika

TEA: Apricot, calendula, jasmine, coriander

SACRAL CHAKRA AFFIRMATIONS

I embrace the journey that is life

With an open heart and an open mind.

I allow my emotions to flow

Through me in a healthy way.

I feel good about myself.

I feel great about my life.

I feel emotionally healthy.

I feel emotionally vibrant.

I feel beauty all around me.

All the beauty that I see, Is a reflection of me.

I feel beautiful.

I am beautiful.

I am vibrant energy and divine love.

I am cosmic bliss and universal light.

Every breath brings me bliss.

Every breath brings me light.

I feel good about myself.

I feel great about my life.

I embrace my creative gifts and talents.

I feel great when I create.

I feel bliss when I share my gifts.

I use my creativity to heal myself.

I use my creativity to help others heal.

I feel good when I play.

I feel joy when I dance.

I embrace my body.

I accept my body.

I embrace my masculine and feminine energies.

I express them in a healthy way.

I feel strong and confident.

I feel sensual and nurturing.

I love to dream.

I love to imagine.

I allow my inner child to roam free.

I allow my soul to dance and explore.

Life is a beautiful journey.

I embrace my role in this cosmic play.

I feel the presence of Spirit all around me.

I feel the protection of my ancestors all around me.

I feel nurtured. I feel supported. I feel cared for.

I explore my purpose. I embrace my purpose.

I feel purposeful.

I release all that does not serve me.

I release trauma, it is not mine.

I release anxiety, it is not mine.

I release depression, it is not mine.

I release attachments, nothing is mine.

I forgive the past and embrace my future.

I release guilt. I release blame. I forgive.

I am forgiven. I embrace all that is.

I embrace all that can be.

I feel free to be myself.

I embrace myself.

I feel free. I feel free. I feel free.

Never invite pain or suffering into your life, but when it comes, hold space for it. Embrace it and receive it as a gift that leads to deeper healing and continued awakening.

POINTS OF DAILY INTROSPECTION

At the start of each day, the spiritual aspirant takes care to make it a habit to practice impartial introspection. While viewing themselves with the soul's love and wisdom, inquire as to things that limit and suppress the expression of their highest nature. The following is a short list of introspective prompts that you may reflect upon during your morning meditation or journaling sessions.

- Where are my emotions centered?

- How often do I check in with my emotional body?

- Are there any toxic feelings/emotions that I may be harboring?

- What has caused these feelings?

- Why do I have an urge to hold on to them?

- What can I do today to release at least one emotional burden?

- What can I create to help me heal?

- What can I do to improve my mood?

- Where is my happy place?

- How often do I go there?

POINTS OF NIGHTLY INTROSPECTION

At the end of each day, the spiritual aspirant takes care to make it a habit to impartially introspect on that day's activities. Nightly introspection allows one to see whether they made spiritual progress and remained committed to the tasks, goals, and intentions established at the start of the day. Writing these things in a spiritual diary allows us to clearly see our repetitive faults and our virtues and make adjustments wherever needed. The following is a short list of introspective prompts that you may reflect upon during or after your nightly meditation.

- How has emotional trauma affected my life?

- What can I do to help myself heal?

- Have I yet to forgive those who may have hurt me?

- Have I yet to show compassion and forgive myself?

- Did any old emotions and hurt resurface today?

- What emotional burdens do I want to release tonight?

- Are there any emotions that may be stopping me from attaining my goals? What are they?

- How do I feel when I have a productive day?

- What inspires me?

EMBRACING YOURSELF
CAN ALSO LOOK LIKE:

- Dancing
- Mirror gazing
- Enjoying alone time
- Verbally thanking your body
- Giving yourself a hug
- Journaling your feelings
- Writing songs/poems about you
- Writing or speaking affirmations

- Buying yourself something that serves your goals
- Taking photos of yourself
- Expressing how you feel
- Treating yourself to a spa day
- Taking a bubble bath or hot shower
- Surrounding yourself with loving people

Everything you love and admire
about the universe is a reminder of
all that you are.

SELF-CARE CHECK-IN

Sit briefly with the following questions; they will determine if you need to tune in and align with the balanced energy of the solar plexus.

- Lately, have you been feeling lazy and uninspired?

- Do you feel you are without purpose?

- Have you been lacking focus and discipline?

- Do you fail to celebrate yourself?

- Have you had great ideas that you've failed to act on lately?

- Have you recently been angry and violent toward others?

- Have you been overeating lately?

- Do you struggle with overcoming an addiction?

- Are you afraid to pursue your dreams and passions?

- Are you lacking confidence?

- Has fear and anxiety taken control of your life lately?

- Do you spend way too much time in idle activities?

- Have others called you controlling?

- Do you lack boundaries in your relationships?

After checking in with yourself, are you satisfied with the answers you gave to the questions above? Do you see where you need some help? This is where the shift starts to happen, and you begin to consciously understand and master your energy. If your answers to the questions above were unsatisfactory to you, this is an indication to focus on the solar plexus today. You can find the Solar Plexus Sadhana in the following chapter. The practice should take you no more than an hour, but there are also auxiliary practices and exercises you may do to further balance the energy in the solar plexus. If you are working on this center, please try not to mix the practices from other chapters with it. The more focus you place on a particular center, the more that energy awakens, and the stronger it becomes. Allow yourself to focus solely on honoring yourself today. Step into your personal power and celebrate the gift of your existence. You are here to do something.

It is such a wonder that the universe has chosen you to be a vessel for its love, creativity, and beauty to be made manifest in human form. Honor your existence by celebrating your uniqueness. You are so worthy and blessed to be you.

HONOR YOURSELF:
SOLAR PLEXUS
OVERVIEW

Each and every one of us is here to create and do something truly profound. We have all been sent forth into this realm of existence to express and embody the wisdom, beauty, love, bliss, and power of the Supreme Intelligence. Supreme Intelligence, Cosmic Consciousness, or God expresses itself through various methods and mediums. Through art, dance, poetry, music, business, science, astrology, mathematics, literature, architecture, and all avenues of service, the Infinite Consciousness plays. You are a spark of infinite consciousness, a vessel of its knowledge and boundless power—and all that it is, you are. Regardless of what you will experience and have endured, nothing will ever deprive you of or distort the image of what you truly are. Life is writing a story through you, and nobody but you can tell it. It is a melody that only you can sing, a dream that only you can see. It is your power and the gift that has been given to you to share with the world.

Accepting and stepping into your personal power is a pivotal point in the journey of healing, growth, and spiritual evolution. Your personal power is everything that makes you, you: your uniqueness, your personality, your passions, your perspective, and your life experiences. No one can live your life. No one can replace you. For the rest of eternity, there will only be one of you. Honoring yourself helps you find your unique place in the infiniteness of the cosmos and allows you to progress confidently into the achievement of your highest goals and ambitions. Angels gather in celebration whenever we step into our personal power. It is an indication that we are growing, blooming, and blossoming into the next phase of our evolution.

ALONG MY JOURNEY

Confidence is something that I've never struggled with, but throughout my life, I have been known to be shy, timid, and somewhat bashful. This may have been partly due to my upbringing or partially due to my earthy nature. Who knows, but I've never been one to celebrate or even honor myself. Growing up, I disliked having birthday parties or being commemorated at school and at home for any academic accomplishments. Whenever someone complimented me on my appearance, achievements, or creativity, I always found a way to deflect their comments. Awkward silence or immediate compliments in return were usually my way of taking the attention away from myself and avoiding any further celebratory remarks.

Because I wasn't willing to honor myself and recognize my personal power, I disliked being celebrated and honored by my peers, family members, or anyone who saw in me what I frequently failed to acknowledge within myself. Now that I've accepted and stepped into my fullness, I realize the value of honoring yourself. I recognize the uniqueness of this embodied state in which I dwell, and I honor the divine life that has chosen to express itself through me. When I honor myself, I honor and celebrate the greatness of God. It's not about me solely; it's about the intelligence that creates through me, serves through me, and shows up in the world as me. This supreme intelligence flows through all of us in infinite ways, and the more we honor it, the more beautiful and fulfilling this experience grows to be.

ABOUT THIS CHAKRA

The Sanskrit name for the solar plexus chakra is Manipuri. The literal translation of Manipuri is "The city of jewels." It is the abode in which we find the gems of wisdom, clarity, spiritual vigor, and self-control. The Manipuri chakra is located in the spine just behind the navel region. It is associated with the color yellow, the element of fire, and is symbolically represented by a lotus flower with ten petals. This center governs our sense of sight and is associated with the feet. The Manipuri chakra is traditionally seen as a place in which masculine energy and our personal power resides. When our energies are grounded, and our emotions are balanced, it is now time to take action, and the fiery energy of the solar plexus chakra inspires us to do just that. This center is characterized by the positive attributes of confidence, passion, drive, ambition, bravery, fearlessness, courage, and a dynamic willpower. When this chakra is open and active, we become trailblazers on the path to both material and spiritual success. After addressing and overcoming our fears, insecurities, and emotional blockages in the lower centers, the rising energy reaches the Manipuri chakra and ignites a flame within us that illuminates our path with passion and a greater sense of purpose.

Mental fortitude, drive, and determination are signs of a healthy and balanced Manipuri chakra. Here, we learn to transmute our pain into progress. We stop playing the victim role and start to take full ownership of our past actions and accept full control of the trajectory of our lives. We no longer sit and wait for things to happen, for people to change, or for circumstances to change. Instead, we go out and create change and be the people we want others to be. Full of confidence and courage, we break down the barriers of shyness, nervousness, self-ridicule, and self-doubt. The sun's energy that resides in the solar plexus illumines us with newfound happiness, self-empowerment, and an unshakable will to succeed.

For the spiritual aspirant, this is the center in which self-control is mastered. Without self-control, it is impossible to progress on the spiritual path, as the world is full of enticing beauty and captivating lures. When tormented by sensual pleasures, material desires, and a fickle mind, we can allow ourselves to be easily drawn away from our spiritual aims. If you control the senses, you control the mind. If you control the mind, you control your fate. Self-control is not self-torture but instead leads to self-mastery and soul liberation. The fire of self-control grants us the mental strength and fortitude necessary to burn away obstacles on our path. These obstacles may be attachment, laziness, addiction, lack of focus, overeating, or the inability to keep the body still during meditation. Self-control is not about imposing our will upon people and things; it is about gaining control of our own energies, being a master of our bodily kingdom, and allowing the pure light of our souls to guide our every action.

The sun of self-mastery rises in the Manipuri chakra and propels us deeper into our spiritual practices. It teaches us that we must do everything with fire. That we must pray with the yearning of fire. Serve with the passion of fire. Meditate with the intensity of fire. And live and walk through life with the *blazing confidence of fire*. When your soul's afire with the definiteness of purpose, self-control, determination, and concentration, you are well on your way toward the summit of success and soul-realization.

SIGNS OF BALANCE
AND IMBALANCE

When your solar plexus is open or balanced, you may feel or experience the following:

Assertive
Confident
Focused
Successful
Productive

Pure happiness
Self-empowered
Self-controlled
Purpose driven

Cooperative and flexible
Ability to make decisions

When your solar plexus is blocked or imbalanced, you may feel or experience the following:

Anger
Shyness
Laziness
Controlling
Aggressiveness

Indecisiveness
Addictions
Low self-esteem
Inability to focus
Lack of ambition

Lack of self-control
Codependency
Fear of rejection
Lack of self-respect

Physical signs and symptoms of imbalances in the solar plexus may also include:

Poor digestion
Hypoglycemia
Diabetes

Asthma
Arthritis
Liver and kidney problems

Nerve pain
Difficulty gaining or losing weight

SOLAR PLEXUS SADHANA

AFFIRMATION

"I am a divine flame of purpose.
I burn with poise, passion, and persistence.
Everything I touch prospers."

MEDITATION:

Listen to the "Honor Yourself: Solar Plexus Meditation."

Available on streaming apps and YouTube.

EXERCISE:

Visualize yourself two years from now. Where would you like to be?
What have you achieved? After the visualization, do something today
that takes you a step closer to making this dream a reality.

SOLAR PLEXUS POSE

When the fire that resides in the navel center is ignited, we develop poise, discipline, self-control, and steadiness of mind. Navasana or boat pose is an asana that stimulates the Manipuri chakra and helps us awaken these virtues while we are on the mat. With our core engaged, legs and arms up in the air as we are seated, the pose challenges us to bring stability to both the body and mind. As we maintain and hold this pose with intensity, our willpower increases and we strengthen our ability to focus and concentrate on any task. Navasana also helps stimulate the digestive fire, helping us assimilate food more efficiently and convert it into revitalizing energy.

BENEFITS

| Strengthens core | Improves discipline | Strengthens willpower |
| Aids in stress relief | Helps with self-control | Improves digestion |

HOW TO DO NAVASANA (BOAT POSE)

1. While in a seated position, place your hands on the mat by your thighs. Bend your knees and place your feet flat on the floor.

2. Bring your feet up off the floor, keeping your knees half bent at first.

3. As your torso naturally falls back, keep your spine straight. Do not let it round.

4. Lift your hands up and stretch them out toward your knees.

5. Unbend your knees and straighten your legs a bit more, while also engaging your core and maintaining balance.

6. Stay here for at least six breaths.

7. Slowly lower your feet, legs, and hands to the floor on the last exhale.

8. Relax and release any tension from your core, hips, hamstrings, and glutes.

9. Try repeating this three to six times to get the full benefits of this pose. Feel free to flow into any other asanas that complement today's practice.

Asanas that balance the solar plexus:

Warrior I
(Virabhadrasana)

Warrior II Pose
(Virabhadrasana II)

Warrior III
(Virabhadrasana III)

Crescent Lunge
(Anjaneyasana)

Chair Pose
(Utkatasana)

Downward Dog
(Adho Mukha
Svanasana)

Full Boat Pose
(Paripurna
Navasana)

Half Lord of the
Fishes Pose (Ardha
Matsyendrasana)

Plank Pose
(Phalakasana)

Child's pose
(Balasana)

Reverse Plank
(Purvottanasana)

Revolved Abdomen
Pose (Jathara
Parivartanasana)

REMINDER

What you are now is the result of what you have practiced in the past. What you will be in the future is the result of what you practice and perform in the present. All that has come to you has been sent to you by the you of the past. All that will come to you is being sent to you by the you of the present. The best way to shape the future is to create it in the present. Fate is none other than the result of present self-effort and present action. We are the designers of our own destinies and the architects of our own fate. Develop your willpower by staying committed to your goals, plans, intentions, and spiritual practice.

Never put off until tomorrow what you can and must do today. We often find that the more we put things off until tomorrow, tomorrow never seems to come. Procrastination weakens your willpower. This results in laziness, demotivation, lack of ambition, and, eventually, failure. You can strengthen your will through persistent self-effort and by striving daily to overcome any bad habits you have allowed yourself to form. To honor yourself also means to honor your goals, intentions, and ambitions by staying committed to them. To dishonor your dreams is to denounce your soul and its power. When your intentions are aligned with your actions and are backed by the fire of willpower, there is nothing that you cannot do or attain.

SOLAR PLEXUS AUXILIARY PRACTICES

In this section, you will find additional exercises, tips, and readings that can be implemented in today's routine. The exercises can be done in any particular order, at any point in time during the day. To stay in alignment with the work within this theme, it is best to practice these exercises on the days that you have chosen to focus on your root chakra. However, it is okay to practice any of these exercises whenever you feel inclined to do so.

SOLAR PLEXUS MANTRA: RAM

The Bija or seed mantra for the solar plexus is RAM.

HOW TO PRACTICE

1. In a seated or standing position, focus your mind's attention to the location of the solar plexus. (In the spine, directly behind the navel.) Close your eyes, feel and visualize a vibrant yellow light glowing at this center.

2. Inhale to the count of six, and as you do so, imagine that the yellow sphere of light is increasing in size.

3. Hold your breath until the count of three. While you do so, maintain the feeling and visualization of the yellow ball of light radiating in the navel region.

4. Exhale, and as you do so, chant RAM (as in rum). Visualize the light becoming smaller and finally being absorbed into this energy center. With your attention still focused on the solar plexus, rest here for twelve seconds and repeat this exercise two more times.

5. If the breathing counts are too long or short for you, feel free to adjust to accommodate your lung capacity. Do not hold your breath for extreme periods of time, as you may cause damage to your lungs, heart, or brain. As a rule of thumb, the length of time you hold your breath can be twice, or half, the length of your inhale.

TIP: If you inhale to the count of six, hold the breath for a three count.Or if you inhale to the count of six, hold the breath to the count of twelve. I do not recommend holding the breath for more than thirty seconds. Be smart! Be safe!

SOLAR PLEXUS MUDRA

SAMANA VAYU MUDRA

Samana Vayu Mudra is a powerful mudra that helps us bring the Manipuri chakra's energies under control. This mudra is also used to ignite and balance the digestive fire, improve self-confidence, clarity, and our ability to make precise and definite decisions.

HOW TO PRACTICE

To perform this mudra, sit in any position with your hands facing upward on your thighs. Close your eyes and focus your attention on the navel region of your body. Bring your pinky finger, ring finger, middle finger, and index finger to touch the tip of your thumbs. All of your fingers (on one hand) should be touching. Do this with both hands with your attention focused on the navel center while performing the following pranayama exercise.

SOLAR PLEXUS

SOLAR PLEXUS PRANAYAMA EXERCISE

1. While performing the Samana Vayu Mudra, bring yourself to a seated position. Focus your mind's attention on the location of the solar plexus. (In the spine, just behind the navel.) Throw the breath out in a double exhalation, "Huh-huh."

2. Inhale completely and fill the belly with prana.

3. Without holding the breath, exhale completely and allow this energy to flow out of the solar plexus and back down to the base of your spine.

4. As you come to the end of the exhale, mentally or verbally say, " I am fire."

5. Allow a brief pause, inhale, and repeat this exercise for ten minutes.

Keep coming back to your breath during the day. To remember your breath is to remember God. To remember God is meditation.

90

SELF-CARE PACKAGE: HEALING THROUGH THE CHAKRAS

SOLAR PLEXUS CRYSTALS

The following is a list of crystals you may use to help stimulate the solar plexus. These crystals may be worn as jewelry, kept in your purse or pocket, or placed on your desk or yoga mat during practice. You can even place them in your bathtub as you soak and take a nice relaxing bath. There are no hard rules as to when and how you can use crystals; just have fun including them in your practice.

Citrine:

Heals digestive system; purifies aura; enhances mental clarity; enhances personal power; increases energy and drive; heightens imagination; promotes self-esteem, courage, creativity, confidence, concentration, and open-mindedness

Golden Apatite:

Promotes optimism and hope; balances appetite; heals eating disorders; strengthens digestive fire; treats depression; fights fatigue and laziness; helps eliminate overactivity and underactivity; helps with concentration

Pyrite:

Helps cure physical infections; heals inertia; purifies blood; balances energetic field; removes dark thoughts; promotes fearlessness; attracts wealth and prosperity; enhances willpower; stimulates ambition, vitality, motivation, and commitment

Lemon Quartz:

Enhances focus; aids in deep meditation; brings clarity, creativity, and optimism; promotes self-control and discipline; strengthens communication skills

SOLAR PLEXUS

Yellow Jasper:

Helps with digestion and stomach issues; eases stress; helps release toxins from the body; brings courage; promotes vitality, self-confidence, tenacity, endurance, and self-transformation

Yellow Topaz:

Helps with memory loss, liver problems, insomnia, and aggressiveness; brings fulfillment of material desires; provides clarity and calmness of mind; promotes happiness, kindness, honesty, and dedication

SOLAR PLEXUS AROMATHERAPY

The following is a list of essential oil, candle, or incense that you may use to stimulate and balance the solar plexus.

Sandalwood	Orange	Rose
Ylang-ylang	Tangerine	Rosemary
Neroli	Geranium	Jasmine

SOLAR PLEXUS JUICE

"SOLAR POWER"

The name says it all! If you're looking for an energy boost or a vibrational shift, this juice is designed to stimulate the Manipuri chakra and bring an increase in vitality, enthusiasm, clarity, and mental alertness. Solar Power charges the body, making you feel rejuvenated and ready for action! It also improves the mood and brings feelings of excitement, playfulness, confidence, and happiness.

Ingredients

3½ Cups of diced honeydew	1 Orange (peeled)	⅛ Tbsp of cayenne pepper
2 Cups of diced pineapples	40 ml of Lemon juice (1 lemon)	

DIRECTIONS

6. Working in this order, process the honeydew, pineapple, finally the peeled orange through a juicer according to the manufacturer's directions.
(No juicer? See Tip.)

7. Add to juice 40 ml of freshly squeezed lemon juice (The equivalent of 1 lemon).

8. Pour juice into a 16-oz. glass or mason jar and stir in 1/8 tbsp of cayenne pepper.

TIP: If you don't have a juicer, place the diced honeydew, pineapples, and peeled orange into your blender, and add 6–8 oz. of alkaline water. After blending, over a large bowl, pour the contents into a nut-milk bag. Squeeze the bag until all the liquid has been removed from the bag and only the fiber remains. Discard the fiber, and carefully pour the juice from the bowl into a glass or mason jar. Add to the juice 40 ml of lemon juice and stir in ⅛ tbsp of cayenne pepper.

Drink on an empty stomach to get the most health benefits.

BENEFITS

Improves immune health	Supports eye health	Aids in muscle recovery
Alkalizes the body	Improves digestion	Improves skin health
Promotes happiness	Eases back and joint pain	
Restores energy	Regulates blood pressure	

SOLAR PLEXUS FOODS

The following is a list of foods that help stimulate the solar plexus. Feel free to include them in your diet on the days in which you focus on this center.

VEGETABLES: Corn, squash, yellow peppers, yellow potatoes, golden beets, pumpkin, yellow beans

FRUITS: Lemon, yellow apples, yellow figs, pineapples, yellow pears, cantaloupe, bananas, starfruit

HERBS: Dandelion, calendula, chamomile, helichrysum, ginger

TEA: Ginger, rosemary, lemon, marshmallow root, fennel

SOLAR PLEXUS AFFIRMATIONS

I will honor my life by doing the best that I can do.

I will honor my soul by being the very best that I can be.

There is no need to be anyone else but myself.

I am worthy of being celebrated.

I am worthy of being appreciated.

I am worthy of being honored.

I honor my existence by sharing my uniqueness.

I appreciate my uniqueness.

I celebrate my uniqueness.

I am proud of my confidence.

I commend myself for being

Strong, persistent, and resilient.

I give myself credit for making it this far.

It is an honor to achieve the things I have achieved.

It is a blessing to accomplish the things I will accomplish.

I will accomplish all that I set out to do.

I am confident in my abilities.

I appreciate and honor my gifts and talents.

I will honor my place in the world by doing what I love.

I will honor my place in creation by serving And celebrating others.

When I win, the world wins.

When the world wins, I win.

I am so happy to be alive.

I wouldn't trade my life for all the world's riches.

I am wealthy in spirit.

I am rich in peace.

I am abundant in Nature.

I honor life with gratitude.

Every moment matters.

I radiate my power in the world.

My presence is felt. My presence is honored.

My life is important.

I can do anything I put my mind to.

I can do anything I invest my time into.

Success is already mine. I claim it.

Abundance is already mine. I claim it.

I am disciplined. I am self-controlled.

I am divine.

I honor and celebrate my divinity.

Enjoy your valleys just as much as you enjoy your peaks.

POINTS OF DAILY INTROSPECTION

At the start of each day, the spiritual aspirant makes it a habit to practice impartial introspection. While viewing themselves with the soul's love and wisdom, inquire as to things that limit and suppress the expression of their highest nature. The following is a short list of introspective prompts that you may reflect upon during your morning meditation or journaling sessions.

- When was the last time I celebrated myself?

- What can I do today to honor my existence?

- What things inspire me to stay committed?

- When I'm having a bad day, what can I do to turn it around?

- How can I ensure that I stay motivated throughout the day?

- What bad habits take me away from my goals?

- What good habits take me toward my goals?

- In what ways can I celebrate or support others?

- How do I feel when I support others?

POINTS OF NIGHTLY INTROSPECTION

At the end of each day, the spiritual aspirant makes it a habit to impartially introspect on that day's activities. Nightly introspection allows one to see whether they made spiritual progress and remained committed to the tasks, goals, and intentions established at the start of the day. Writing these things in a spiritual diary allows us to clearly see our repetitive faults and our virtues and make adjustments wherever needed. The following is a short list of introspective prompts that you may reflect upon during or after your nightly meditation.

- In the battle between my good and bad habits, which side won today?

- Am I satisfied with this answer?

- In what ways can I improve or better myself after today?

- Did I honor my commitments today?

- Did I allow anything or anyone to cause me to have an unproductive today?

- How do I feel when I get things accomplished?

- What can I do to build on my daily accomplishments?

- Did I take the time to appreciate where I am today?

HONORING YOURSELF CAN ALSO LOOK LIKE:

- Waking up on time
- Going to sleep earlier
- Setting healthy boundaries
- Knowing when and how to say no
- Volunteering
- Eating healthier
- Socializing with others
- Sharing your gifts and talents
- Sharing your story
- Spending time alone

- Rewarding yourself with gifts
- Taking breaks from technology
- Practicing self-control
- Sticking to your commitments
- Being more organized
- Celebrating your accomplishments
- Celebrating and appreciating others

Your heart is a portal into love.

SELF-CARE CHECK-IN

Sit briefly with the following questions; they will determine if you need to tune in and align with the balanced energy of the heart chakra.

- Have you poured into you lately?

- Does your heart feel full?

- Does your heart feel blocked or heavy in any way?

- Do you have a hard time allowing life to do its part?

- Do you feel like you're in a rush to accomplish something?

- Are you struggling to let go of heartbreak?

- Do you fear rejection or seek approval?

- Are you resisting or rejecting love from others?

- Do you feel loved by others?

- Does love feel distant, unattainable, or foreign to you?

- Have you been reluctant to trust others?

- Do you feel disconnected from you?

- Do you need to release something?

- Do you want to feel and understand love?

After checking in with yourself, how satisfied are you with the answers you gave to the questions above? This is where the shift starts to happen, and you begin to consciously understand and master your energy. If your answers to the questions above were unsatisfactory to you, this is an indication to focus on the heart chakra today. You can find the Heart Chakra Sadhana in the following chapter. The practice should take you no more than an hour, but there are also auxiliary practices and exercises you may do to further balance the energy in the heart chakra. If you are working on this center, please try not to mix the practices from other chapters with it. The more focus you place on a particular center, the more that energy awakens, and the stronger it becomes. Allow yourself to walk into and lead with love today. Let love inspire everything you do. Let love greet you in everyone you see and meet.

When love is your vibration, your energy is your protection.

LOVE YOURSELF:
HEART CHAKRA
OVERVIEW

Self-love is often mistakenly taken to mean vanity, selfish pride, self-indulgence, or selfishness. Self-love is a spiritual endeavor that allows us to break free from the limitations that these qualities impose upon the soul. It grants us the ability to experience the full spectrum and power of love. We often start the journey into self-love because of heartbreak, our discontent with life, or beautiful quotes and heartfelt songs written on the subject. But self-love is more than a mender of broken hearts; it is an elixir and healer of life. It is a portal into understanding the cosmos and an exploration that allows us to experience the universe within our very own being.

Every human being is a reflection of the creation in which he or she dwells. Within you, there are worlds of knowledge, infinite dimensions of wisdom, galaxies of love, and solar systems of profound power. You are the universe expressing itself in human form, and your life is life's way of communicating with itself. When you love yourself, you are entering your own personal universe and discovering the hidden secrets of the microcosm within. As within, so without. When these loving energies are directed inward, you gradually awaken to the nature of your soul and the nature of creation. To understand the life within you is to understand the life around you. Loving yourself leads to the expansion of knowledge and realization of the soul. But this love does not end with you. It leads you to realize that everything is you and awakens you to universal love—the love that includes all, embraces all, and loves all.

We love ourselves so that we can become vessels for Divine Love to be expressed and felt in this dimension. In a world that is spiritually starving due to the lack of love, it is our duty to transform ourselves through love's power and offer that same love to hungry hearts all over. Love expands the mind, satisfies the heart, and liberates the soul. In love, we dissolve ourselves in God. With hearts immersed in God, we are better equipped to serve in our communities, in our homes, in our relationships, and in all of our endeavors.

ALONG MY JOURNEY

Like many of us, my journey into the awareness and importance of self-love started after heartbreak. Before then, I had no clue how much I lacked genuine love and appreciation for myself. This trait not only caused me to devalue myself, but it also resulted in me not offering love to the relationship in a way that supported its continued growth and expansion. At the time, I admit I wasn't nurturing myself, and so I attracted a partner who was neither nurturing themselves nor was able to provide a nurturing space in the relationship. I also hadn't taken the time to really get to know and heal myself. Thus, that resulted in me being in a relationship with someone who had no deep interest in understanding themselves or allowed themselves space to heal from their past traumatic experiences. Our relationship ended in the most violent and volatile way—with me in the ER as a victim of gun violence.

Perhaps this was the karma of our toxic exchange, or maybe it was the only thing that would prompt me to completely walk away from the relationship. Of course, I did, and despite the negative impact of this horrific and traumatic experience, it sparked a significant shift and change in my life. After this, I became more interested in why I was the way I was. Why was I hurt? Why was I broken? Why did I feel worthless and unlovable? These were all questions that inspired my inward journey. It probably wasn't the best way of going about it, but I shut myself off to relationships, most friendships, and any connection with the outside world. As I closed the doors of my heart to others, I opened up to myself. The first few years of this were painful, lonely, and antagonizing. But as I became a friend and lover to myself, all of that darkness within was transformed into light. This book is filled with things I learned and did to shift my consciousness and open my heart—from which I am still learning, evolving, and healing.

ABOUT THIS CHAKRA

The Sanskrit name for the heart chakra is Anāhata. The literal translation of Anāhata is "unhurt, unstruck, and unbeaten." The Anāhata or heart chakra is located in the spine just behind the center of the chest. It is symbolically depicted as a lotus flower with twelve petals and is represented by the element of air. It is also associated with the color green and is responsible for our sense of touch. The twelve lotus petals of the heart chakra symbolically represent the twelve qualities of the heart. They are love, joy, bliss, peace, patience, harmony, clarity, compassion, kindness, purity, understanding, and forgiveness. The heart center is the bridge between our higher and lower selves. In this chakra, the passion of the solar plexus is transmuted into compassion, and the emotion that powers the sacral center evolves into devotion. Through the awakening of divine love, compassion, and devotion, we ascend from the lower states of consciousness into the heart and gradually become aware of the boundless nature of our beings. Just as the entire tree is present already in the seed, the essence of the entire cosmos is present in the seat of the heart chakra.

The ancients say that the heart chakra is the seat of the soul, our personal identity. The soul is not different from God or Cosmic Consciousness. It, too, is eternal, unborn, undying, ever-existing, all-knowing, all-powerful, and boundless. When the heart center is open and fully explored, we experience an overwhelming sense of joy, satisfaction, bliss, and love. This experience is none other than the direct or conscious perception of the soul. Love, whether it be directed outwardly or inwardly, allows us to feel and experience a new dimension of ourselves. Wherever we direct our love is where we will find a greater understanding of who and what we are. Just as the soul is infinite, so is the power of love that radiates from the heart center. This is why we use phrases such as "I have a big heart" or "Have room in your heart for everyone." Love, too, is ever expanding, and the moment we attempt to close the doors of our heart, we disallow this expansion and, as a result, halt all spiritual progress.

As the heart opens, the more sensitive and emotionally empathetic we become. We expand in our capacity to feel both spiritual bliss and subtle spiritual pain. This pain may not only be a result of things we have experienced in this life, but it may also be the resurfacing of painful experiences from past lives as well. This is why it is important to keep the heart open. When we close off the heart out of fear of being hurt or mistreated further, we block the heart and disallow its healing energies to flow throughout our threefold body matrix.

In essence, all love is Self-Love, but when the energy of love is directed inward, it cleanses and renews the heart, bringing fresh new life, inspiration, and rejuvenation to the spirit and allows us to consciously experience our own love. To consciously experience your own love is both therapeutic and liberating. Self-love heals the deepest wounds and removes the most abrasive insecurities. Self-love liberates and releases us from the grips of painstaking memories of past hurt, failure, and traumatic experiences.

Your love is a portal into you. When you enter this portal, you are granted access to all versions of you and given the power to heal the past and everyone in it. To love yourself is to bring harmony and heaven into your heart. When heaven is in your heart, there will also be the bliss and power of God.

SIGNS OF BALANCE AND IMBALANCE

When your heart chakra is open or balanced, you may feel or experience the following:

Selfless
Joyful
Peaceful
Generous
Empathetic
Trusting
Forgiving

Nurturing
Devotion
Self-surrendering
Emotionally stable
Harmony in relationships
Compassion for all

life
Able to give and receive love
Compassion for Self and others

When your heart chakra is blocked or imbalanced, you may feel or experience the following:

Grief
Greed
Selfishness
Resentment
Arrogance
Unloved
Lack of empathy
Lack of compassion

Inability to forgive
Possessive attitude
Lacking discrimination
Unwilling to forgive
Inability to receive love
Lack of self-love

Heavyhearted
Argumentative
Guarded heart
Emotionally unavailable
Emotionally disconnected

Physical signs and symptoms of imbalances in the heart chakra may also include:

Chest pain
Pain in hands
Shoulder tightness

High blood pressure
Low blood pressure

Heart problems
Lung difficulties

HEART CHAKRA SADHANA

AFFIRMATION

"As I love myself, I consciously awaken my power to self-heal."

MEDITATION

Listen to the "Love Yourself: Heart Chakra Meditation."
Available on streaming apps and YouTube.

EXERCISE

What does love mean to you? Write a poem
or draw a picture that captures this feeling.

POSE OF THE DAY

BHUJANGASANA (COBRA POSE)

Learning to lead with our hearts in moments that call for the expression of compassion, empathy, emotional availability, and softness is vital to both individual and interpersonal growth. Bhujangasana or cobra pose is an asana that inspires us to lead our lives with an open heart and a willingness to expand in love. Cobra pose helps open up the chest and increase the flow of prana throughout the heart and lungs. As the prana, or life force, flows freely through these organs, it stimulates the Anāhata chakra and brings balance and restoration to the heart center. Bhujangasana also brings stimulation to the entire spine, thereby encouraging the activation of the five chakras that are located in the spine. Just a few moments spent doing this pose will invoke feelings of love and help relieve stress, anxiety, and emotional grief.

BENEFITS

Elevates mood	Stimulates the spine	Relieves stress and fatigue
Strengthens spine	Helps breathing	
Opens the heart	difficulties	

HOW TO DO BHUJANGASANA (COBRA POSE)

1. Lay flat on your mat with your thighs and feet pressed firmly on the floor.

2. Bend your elbow and place the palms of both hands just underneath your shoulders.

3. Inhale gently, and as you do so, push yourself up and extend both arms.

4. Your abdomen should be off the mat while your pelvis, thighs, knees, and feet remain firmly planted.

5. As you extend the arms, open your chest by pushing both shoulder blades to the center of your back.

6. Elongate your neck and allow your back to bend naturally.

7. Try not to overextend your spine by bending too far back or straining your neck.

8. At the top of the inhale, hold for six seconds and as you exhale, return to the starting position.

9. Try repeating this three to six times to get the full benefits of this pose. Feel free to flow into any other asanas that complement today's practice.

Asanas that balance the heart chakra:

Melting Heart Pose (Anahatasana)

Sphinx Pose (Salamba Bhujangasana)

Cobra Pose (Bhujangasana)

Upward-Facing Dog (Urdhva Mukha Svanasana)

Low Lunge (Anjaneyasana)

High Lunge (Utthita ashwa sanchalanasana)

Tree Pose (Vrksasana)

Dancers Pose (Natarajasana)

Triangle Pose (Utthita Trikonasana)

Camel pose (Ustrasana)

Fish Pose (Matsyasana)

Bridge Pose (Setu Bandha Sarvangasana)

Corpse Pose (Savasana)

REMINDER

As you grow in love, so shall you grow in life. When the heart expands, the mind expands. When the mind expands, life is filled with abundance, beauty, prosperity, peace, and soul satisfaction. Love is a force that brings healing, happiness, and harmony into every dimension of our lives. Love is the simplicity of water and the profoundness of the cosmos. Love is ever near, and never far. Love is here, and wherever you are. You are love Divine. You are love eternal. You are love ever new. You are boundless love and infinite light. To know yourself is to love yourself. Take every opportunity you have to become more acquainted with the universe within you—with the love within you. This self-inquiring attitude will lead you into a deeper understanding of life, love, and all things divine. Self-love and self-knowledge open us up to universal love. In this love, there is no fear, no hatred, no hurt, no discontent, or sorrow. In the purity of universal love, one realizes that all people, all things, and all life that resides in the universe are not separate from themselves. Enter the portal of self-love and allow it to expand into universal love. Love others just as your love yourself. Love yourself just as you love others.

But why must you love others? To love others is to love yourself. There is nothing but you—everything and everyone is you. In the beginningless beginning, there was only you. You existed as boundless bliss, infinite knowledge, and endless love. As pure consciousness, you knew you were these things, but you wanted to experience yourself as these things. And the instant this idea came into your awareness, you formed the worlds, universes, and all their inhabitants, all out of your own being. Dividing yourself into infinite forms, you sought to love yourself infinitely. Though you appear now to be an individual, you are not. You are still infinite and pure consciousness. Just as in a dream, different dream people sprout up in your consciousness, all seeming to have their own individuality, so too is true in this dream world. Everything and everyone are projections of your own mind—it is all you. Love is a coming back to this understanding and realization. Love is a coming back to you.

HEART CHAKRA AUXILIARY PRACTICES

In this section, you will find additional exercises, tips, and readings that can be implemented in today's routine. The exercises can be done in any particular order, at any point in time during the day. To stay in alignment with the theme of this section, it is best to practice these exercises on the days that you have chosen to focus on your heart chakra. However, it is okay to practice any of these exercises whenever you feel inclined to do so.

HEART CHAKRA MANTRA: YAM

The Bija or seed mantra for the heart chakra is YAM.

HOW TO PRACTICE

1. In a seated or standing position, focus your mind's attention on the location of the heart chakra. (In the spine, just behind the heart.) Close your eyes and visualize a vibrant green light glowing at this center.

2. Inhale to the count of six, and as you do so, imagine that the green sphere of light is increasing in size.

3. Hold your breath until the count of three. While you do so, maintain the visualization of the green ball of light radiating at the base of your spine.

4. Exhale, and as you do so, chant YAM (YUM as in yummy). Visualize the light becoming smaller and finally being absorbed into this energy center.

5. With your attention still focused on the heart chakra, rest here for a few seconds and repeat this exercise 2–6 more times.

6. If the breathing counts are too long or short for you, feel free to adjust to accommodate your lung capacity. Do not hold your breath for extreme periods of time, as you may cause damage to your lungs, heart, or brain. As a rule of thumb, the length of time you hold your breath can be twice, or half, the length of your inhale.

TIP: If you inhale to the count of six, hold the breath for a three count. Or if you inhale to the count of six, hold the breath to the count of twelve. I do not recommend holding the breath for more than thirty seconds. Be smart! Be safe!

HEART CHAKRA MUDRA

HRIDAYA MUDRA

Hridaya mudra, also referred to as the "heart gesture" is a powerful mudra that brings revitalizing and rejuvenating energy to and from the heart center. Hridaya mudra helps heal any heart and respiratory-related issues, induces calmness, reduces body pain, and improves digestion.

HOW TO PRACTICE

To perform this mudra, sit in any position with your palms facing upward on your thighs. Bend the index finger and place it at the base of the thumb. You should be able to feel the pulse. Bring the thumb to touch the tips of the middle and ring fingers. Let the little finger remain up and relaxed. Hold this mudra while you meditate on love or practice the following pranayama exercise.

HEART CHAKRA PRANAYAMA EXERCISE

While performing Hridaya mudra, bring yourself to a comfortable seated position. Focus your mind's attention on the location of the heart chakra. (In the spine, just behind the heart.) Throw the breath out in a double exhalation "Huh-huh."

1. Inhale completely and fill the heart center with prana.

2. Without holding the breath, exhale completely and allow this energy to flow out of the heart chakra and back down to the base of your spine.

3. As you come to the end of the exhale, mentally or verbally affirm, "I am love."

4. Allow a brief pause, inhale, and repeat this exercise for 6–12 minutes.

Air is the element of the heart— breathing is a loving action.

HEART CHAKRA CRYSTALS

Here is a list of crystals you may use to help stimulate the solar plexus. These crystals may be worn as jewelry, kept in your purse or pocket, or placed on your desk or yoga mat during practice. You can even place them in your bathtub as you soak and take a nice relaxing bath. There are no hard rules as to when and how you can use crystals; just have fun including them in your practice.

Rose Quartz:

Heals PTSD; promotes heart and kidney health; reduces high blood pressure; opens heart chakra; invokes love, trust, and self-worth; eases stress and anxiety; stimulates intuition; promotes compassion, forgiveness, self-acceptance, kindness, empathy, and unconditional love.

Emerald:

Improves vision; heals heart, lungs, muscles, and spinal issues; strengthens spiritual insight; helps one adapt to change; cleanses aura; enhances psychic abilities; stimulates intuition, memory, vision, focus, and creativity; promotes abundance, joy, love, truthfulness, and clairvoyance

Rhodonite:

Soothes nervous system; heals inner child, grief, sadness, and depression; generates compassion; heals trauma and family bitterness; clears anger, resentment, and unforgiveness; aids in emotional healing and resolving relationship issues

Green Aventurine:

Supports heart health; helps with fertility; heals eyesight, lungs, and thymus gland; balances emotional body; calms nervousness, anger, and irritation; calms the mind; inspires humor, joy, optimism, and hope

Green Jade:

Heals kidneys, spleen, liver, and balances body fluids; protects from harm; helps release negative energies; helps attract friendship and or love; good luck stone; inspires creative ideas; encourages self-sufficiency

Amazonite:

Heals heart and throat complications; relieves muscle spasms; alleviates stress; helps problem solve; aligns astral body; inspires confidence; brings extra energy to positive affirmations; enhances creative self-expression; promotes peace, harmony, truth, healthy communication, emotional healing, luck, honesty, and prosperity

Prehnite:

Aligns heart and mind; strengthens life force; increases energy; helps release fears, attachments, and phobias; promotes harmony, love, fearlessness, and organization

Malachite:

Aids in healing asthma, arthritis, joint issues, broken bones, and torn muscles; helps with shyness; supports immune health; absorbs pollution; removes attachments; purifies aura; promotes adventure, change, and imagination; stimulates psychic visions, sensuality, and intuition

Chrysoprase:

Cures restlessness; mends a broken heart; strengthens eyes; aids in pain relief; brings success; balances yin and yang energies; brings clarity; banishes greed, selfishness, and carelessness; activates the heart chakra; promotes forgiveness, understanding, happiness, luck, adaptability, joy, hope, and courage

HEART CHAKRA AROMATHERAPY

The following is a list of essential oil, candle, or incense scents that you may use to stimulate and balance the solar plexus:

Mandarin	Cypress	Pine
Ylang-ylang	Geranium	Eucalyptus
Lavender	Rose	

HEART CHAKRA JUICE

"LOVING AWARENESS"

Designed to unblock and open the heart center, this juice increases one's awareness of love, reduces stress, and promotes the release of unhealthy emotions. *Loving Awareness* also brings clarity and expands the mind, allowing you to feel love for all that you are aware of.

Ingredients:

2½ cups of diced pineapples
½ cucumber

2 celery stalks
2 inches of ginger

10 ml of lime juice
⅛ tbsp of spirulina

DIRECTIONS

- Working in this order, process pineapple, cucumber, celery, and ginger through a juicer according to the manufacturer's directions. (No juicer? See Tip.)

- Add to juice 10 ml of freshly squeezed lime juice (The equivalent of ½ lime.)

- Pour juice into a 16-oz. glass or mason jar and stir in ⅛ tbsp of spirulina powder.

TIP: If you don't have a juicer, place the suggested amount of diced pineapples, cucumber, celery, and ginger into your blender, and add 6–8 oz. of alkaline water. After blending, over a large bowl, pour the contents into a nut-milk bag. Squeeze the bag until all the liquid has been removed from the bag and only the fiber remains. Discard the fiber and carefully pour the juice from the bowl into an 8-oz. glass or mason jar. Add to the juice 10 ml of lime juice and stir in 1/8 tbsp of spirulina powder.

Drink on an empty stomach to get the most benefits.

BENEFITS

Anti-aging
Fights cancer
Reduces anxiety

Increases energy
Immune booster
Improves heart health

Anti-inflammatory
Reduces cramps
Removes mucus

HEART CHAKRA FOODS

The list below contains a list of foods that help stimulate the heart chakra. Feel free to include them in your diet on the days in which you focus on this center.

VEGETABLES: Kale, broccoli, spinach, chard, collard greens, dandelion greens, celery, zucchini, brussels sprouts, peas, asparagus, snap peas, snow peas, and garden peas

FRUITS: Kiwi, green apples, green grapes, cucumbers, avocado, lime, greengage plums, guava, soursop, cherimoyas, jackfruit, and gooseberries

HERBS: Coriander, mint, dill, oregano, parsley, thyme, rosemary, tarragon, basil, and sage

TEA: Mint, green tea, Hawthorn, Rosehip, Matcha

HEART CHAKRA AFFIRMATIONS

I feel love within me.

I feel love all around me.

Every day I am becoming more loving and compassionate.

Being kind to others also means being kind to myself.

I appreciate my love. I value my life.

I accept myself for who I am.

I am divine love and radiant light.

I vibrate pure love.

I vibrate radiant light.

My thoughts and desires are

In harmony with universal love.

I love myself unconditionally.

There is nothing that I lack.

I am beautiful inside and out.

I am attractive.

I am abundant.

I am rich in love.

There is no need to be perfect.

Perfection is only an idea, not a reality.

I am self-nurturing.

I am self-caring.

I am self-loving.

The better I take care of myself.

The more help I can offer to others.

My love includes all.

My love embraces all.

I open my heart and release grief.

I open my heart and release resentment.

I open my heart and release judgment.

I open my heart and release jealousy.

I believe in forgiveness.

I practice forgiveness.

I forgive myself.

I forgive all.

I refuse to live
my life with a
heavy heart.

I have love for all.

I forgive all.

I enjoy time alone.

I enjoy time
with others.

Love is my
language.

Love is my breath.

Love is my life.

I love myself.

I love my breath.

I love my life.

I am love eternal.

I am love divine.

I am love here.

I am love now.

**Wealth starts with your
well-being. Take care
of yourself and your health,
and life will take care of you.**

POINTS OF DAILY INTROSPECTION

At the start of each day, the spiritual aspirant makes it a habit to practice impartial introspection. While viewing themselves with the soul's love and wisdom, inquire as to things that limit and suppress the expression of their highest nature. The following is a short list of introspective prompts that you may reflect upon during your morning meditation or journaling sessions.

- What does love mean to me?

- How well do I express these things to myself and others?

- In what ways can I show love to myself today?

- In what ways can I show love to others today?

- How often do I express my appreciation to others?

- How often do I express my gratitude to life?

- What am I devoted to?

- Have I been consistent in my devotion?

POINTS OF NIGHTLY
INTROSPECTION

At the end of each day, the spiritual aspirant makes it a habit to impartially introspect on that day's activities. Nightly introspection allows one to see whether they made spiritual progress and remained committed to the tasks, goals, and intentions established at the start of the day. Writing these things in a spiritual diary allows us to clearly see our repetitive faults and our virtues and make adjustments wherever needed. The following is a short list of introspective prompts that you may reflect upon during or after your nightly meditation.

- Did I lead with love today?

- What were some things that helped me do so?

- What were some things that stopped me from doing so?

- Did I express my love to someone today?

- How did that make me feel?

- Do I feel loved by life?

- What can I do tomorrow to open my heart even more?

- Are there any things that are weighing heavy on my heart?

- What do I need to release?

LOVING YOURSELF
CAN ALSO LOOK LIKE:

- Taking a walk in nature

- Enjoying silence

- Journaling or life planning

- Spending time with your family

- Cooking yourself a nice meal

- Volunteering and serving others

- Creating something just for you

- Dressing up and taking photos

- Listening to your favorite
  love songs

- Expressing your love to others

- Treating yourself to
  something nice

- Spending quality time alone

- Doing yoga or playing a sport

- Doing conscious breathing
  exercises

- Removing yourself from
  hurtful relationships

- Taking a nap after a rough day
  at work

- Reading your favorite book

- Going to the gym and
  working out

- Meditating on love

- Writing affirmations on love

When we realize and accept that God is consciousness, we can develop a deeper appreciation for life and its many expressions—all being a manifestation of consciousness.

SELF-CARE CHECK-IN

Sit briefly with the following questions; they will determine if you need to tune in and align with the balanced energy of the throat chakra.

- Do you feel unheard?

- Do you need to speak to your inner child?

- Do you need to communicate something to yourself?

- Have you been struggling to express yourself creatively?

- Do you struggle with shyness or social anxiety?

- Do you find your speech to be often harsh or cruel?

- Are you preparing for a public speaking event?

- Are you experiencing shoulder or neck pain?

- Do you frequently get into arguments with others?

- Do you find yourself being dishonest or telling small lies?

- Do you want to be better at expressing your feelings?

- Do you want to improve your ability to express your thoughts?

After checking in with yourself, how satisfied are you with the answers you gave to the questions above? This is where the shift starts to happen, and you begin to consciously understand and master your energy. If your answers to the questions above were unsatisfactory to you, this is an indication to focus on the throat chakra today. You can find the Throat Chakra Sadhana in the following chapter. The practice should take you no more than an hour, but there are also auxiliary practices and exercises you may do to further balance the energy in the throat chakra. If you are working on this center, please try not to mix the practices from other chapters with it. The more focus you place on a particular center, the more that energy awakens, and the stronger it becomes. Give yourself permission to commune with your innermost being. Let this lead you into authentic and loving self-expressions.

Every word you speak has a vibratory effect on your body, your being, and your environment. Speak life into life. Speak love and be love.

EXPRESS YOURSELF:
THROAT CHAKRA
OVERVIEW

Every living entity, organism, and individual that dwells in the universe is a living, breathing expression of Spirit, God, or Cosmic Consciousness. The flowers express the beauty of God. The trees express the patience and selflessness of God. The sun expresses the warm nature and radiant light of God. The purity of God is expressed through the swan and dove, and God's wisdom and gentle nature are symbolically manifested in the elephant. Even the foods that we eat and drink express the all-satisfying goodness, sweetness, and savor of God. All that we find in the world of matter is a unique expression of the infinite qualities that reside in Spirit. Though we may not always feel and act as such, human beings are perhaps the most unique expression of God on this plane of existence. Being made in the image of God, we are endowed with the capacity and ability to fully express and embody all that our Creator is. Unlike other life forms that live primarily by instinct, we possess the power of intellect, which allows us to consciously choose our thoughts, words, emotions, and actions. When we do anything consciously, we do it with the power of God, and we do it as an expression of God. To consciously and confidently express yourself is to allow the power, beauty, wisdom, and love of the cosmos to express itself through you. The more comfortable you become with expressing yourself, the more you heal, learn, and grow in all dimensions of your life. You are the cosmos expressing itself in human form. Self-expression leads to self-discovery, self-appreciation, self-fulfillment, and soul-satisfaction.

ALONG MY JOURNEY

As a writer, author, musician, and poet, I know from firsthand experience how the power of words and expressing words can transform one's life. Words in themselves are life. They possess the power to heal, uplift, console, elevate, and grow. Words, for me, are portals into the mysteries and secrets of the soul. They express the vastness of the mind, the immensity of thoughts, the depth of emotions, and the immeasurable beauty of the cosmos. Words allow me to hear and express all that there is to feel, think, and dream. Words are perhaps my greatest friend and companion.

I've always had a way with words, but I haven't always been the wordsmith that I am today. As I mentioned before, I was quite shy and reserved as a child and throughout adolescence. And I must admit, this is why I am a much more proficient writer than I am a speaker. My method of self-expression has always been through writing. Whether it be through poetry, song, or written philosophy, I feel most connected to myself and God when it's just me, a pen, and my notebook. This is how the universe expresses itself through me and how I commune with the God in me. Through my words, I have been able to heal and transform my life and offer healing and transformation to others. I could not dream of any other way to express myself and serve others than through the gift of words.

ABOUT THIS CHAKRA

The Sanskrit name for the throat chakra is Vishuddha. The literal translation of Vishuddha is "especially pure." Located in the spine, directly behind the pit of the throat in the cervical region, the throat chakra is the center of spiritual purification, self-expression, and creativity. The activity of this center is responsible for our best creative work, which includes art, poetry, music, philosophy, theology, theater, and literature. The throat chakra is symbolically represented by a lotus flower with sixteen petals and is associated with the color blue and the element of ether or space. It is responsible for our sense of hearing and our ability to speak. Communication is a major requirement for all interpersonal relationships as well as the relationship we have with ourselves. The Vishuddha chakra, being the center of spiritual purification, requires that we communicate with others in a healthy way. Harsh speech, gossip, lying, and the inability to listen are signs of blockages in this center. The throat chakra is not only influenced by the things we say but also by the things we don't say.

Not speaking up for ourselves or failing to express our emotions are also things that have an adverse influence on the Vishuddha chakra. We must always be willing to express how we feel without fear of being judged or condemned by others. Expressing our deepest feelings and thoughts help us become aware of ourselves, and thus we become more confident and understanding of how we can be better individuals, partners, and or friends.

The Vishuddha chakra, when activated and balanced, acts as a filter for all that is impure, insensitive, and vile. Though this center requires that we speak the truth, if we find that truth is mentally or emotionally injurious to others, we must be self-controlled and discerning enough to compassionately withhold our words. Speaking to intentionally cause harm to another in the end usually does more harm to us than it does to others. Once we speak, those words can never be taken back, so we strive to be mindful and taste our words before we allow them to escape beyond our lips. Words have power, and how we express ourselves is how we communicate that power. You can tell a lot about a person by the words that they choose to speak and how they are spoken. A wise person speaks very smoothly, calmly, intently, and with caution as to not confuse or harm those who may be on the receiving end of their words. A passionate person speaks very sharply, bluntly, and often speaks without measuring the impact of their words as they are spoken. When the energy rises and rests at this center, one gains mastery of words and is able to efficiently speak things into existence.

With the activation and healthy use of the Vishuddha chakra, we are encouraged to speak our truth and express our most authentic selves. Your truth is who you are, your upbringing, the things that you have learned, experienced, and witnessed during the course of your life. The things that make you feel happy, joyous, inspired, and purposeful. Also, the things that cause you sorrow, sadness, and discontent. Speaking your truth and expressing yourself affords you the freedom to be who you are without reserve or self-doubt. Self-expression is how we honor and celebrate God within us. Something profound and amazing wants to be expressed through each of us, and we all have unique gifts to share with the world. As you garner more strength and courage to express yourself, your life is thus filled with all the things you need to allow that beautiful expression to expand and grow.

SIGNS OF BALANCE AND IMBALANCE

When your throat chakra is open or balanced, you may feel or experience the following:

- Calmness
- Empathy
- Intense joy
- The ability to listen
- Purification of mind
- Straightforwardness
- Truthfulness and honesty
- Ease of communication
- Renewed confidence
- Creative expressiveness

When your throat chakra is blocked or imbalanced, you may feel or experience the following:

- Vanity
- Pride
- Shyness
- Dishonesty
- Disloyalty
- Fear of speaking
- Social anxiety
- Lack of creativity
- Lack of self-control
- Harsh or hurtful speech
- Inability to express thoughts

Physical signs and symptoms of imbalances in the throat chakra may also include:

- Neck pain
- Mouth ulcers
- Thyroid issues
- Sore throat
- Laryngitis
- Hoarseness
- Tight jaw

THROAT CHAKRA SADHANA

AFFIRMATION

"I express myself lovingly and allow myself to be a loving expression of the universe."

MEDITATION

Listen to the "Express Yourself: Throat Chakra Meditation."

Available on streaming apps and YouTube.

EXERCISE

While standing in front of a mirror, express to yourself the words you may have been longing to hear, either in the past or the present moment.

POSE OF THE DAY

SIMHASANA (LION POSE)

Simhasana, or lion pose, is a pose that literally imitates the roar of a lion. Despite it being an unusual and not-so-familiar asana, many yoga practitioners use this pose for emotional balance, spiritual upliftment, and mental clarity. Simhasana combines both asana (physical posture) and pranayama (breath control) to produce a deep and resounding lion-like roar during the peak of exhalation. Though at first, it may seem awkward, this pose helps awaken our childlike nature and allows us to feel more lighthearted and vocally confident. Physically, this posture is known to relieve bodily tension, neck pain, and bring relaxation to the face and chest muscles. Emotionally, Simhasana helps boost confidence, release unhealthy feelings, and it helps remove the fears of speaking and being judged by others.

BENEFITS

Eases emotional stress	tension	keeps skin tight
Improves confidence	Decreases nervousness	Beneficial for eye, nose, ear, and
Removes chest	Exercises face and	throat health

HOW TO DO SIMHASANA (LION POSE)

1. Come to a kneeling position with the knees slightly separated.

2. Place your hands on your knees with fingers spread wide.

3. Inhale deeply through the nose while slightly leaning forward and opening the chest.

4. Exhale the breath forcibly out of the mouth.

5. As you exhale open your eyes and mouth while also sticking your tongue out, making the sound "Haaaaaaaaa."

6. Gaze up into the brow chakra as you roar!

7. Try repeating this exercise three to six times to get the full benefits of this pose. Feel free to flow into any other asanas that complement today's practice.

Asanas that balance the throat chakra:

Seated Neck Rolls

Seated Mountain Pose (Parvatasana)

Child's pose (Balasana)

Crocodile Pose (Makarasana)

Cobra Pose (Bhujangasana)

Thunderbolt Pose (Vajrasana)

Cat-Cow Pose (Chakravakasana)

Lion's Breath (Simhasana Pranayama)

Camel Pose (Ustrasana)

Supported Shoulder Stand (Salamba Sarvangasana)

Plow Pose (Halasana)

Bridge Pose (Setu Bhandasana)

Revolved Abdomen pose (Jathara Parivartanasana)

Fish Pose (Matsyasana)

Corpse Pose (Savasana)

REMINDER

Speak up for yourself. Don't be shy about the things you want for your life and those that you love. We don't always get what we want, but we certainly never get what we fail to ask for. If you know in your heart you are worthy and deserving of it, it will come to you without fail. When you pray and affirm yourself, let there be no hesitation, doubt, or feelings of unworthiness in your mind. Quite too often, we talk ourselves out of receiving things because, in some form or fashion, we believe that we aren't worthy of having them. These beliefs are due to a lack-based mindset, which springs from a lack of self-knowledge and the limits of one's own mind. You are a child of the cosmos. It is your Divine birthright to have whatsoever you need to sustain you and help you prosper in life. Get personal with God. His Infinite Kingdom is within you.

Lay all of your needs, wants, and desires on the altar of your heart and ask with confidence, faith, and conviction for anything your life may call for you to have. No dream is too big, and no request is too extravagant for the one who has draped the cosmos with stars, moons, galaxies, and multidimensional universes. If the earth itself is abundantly supplied with diamonds, gold, gems, food, and other valuables, surely the Maker of the universe can grant you all that you require. Never be afraid to ask for what you truly want. When it's spoken from the heart and with soul force, you'll be surprised how easily it comes to you.

THROAT CHAKRA AUXILIARY PRACTICES

In this section, you will find additional exercises, tips, and readings that can be implemented in today's routine. The exercises can be done in any particular order, at any point in time during the day. To stay in alignment with the theme of this section, it is best to practice these exercises on the days that you have chosen to focus on your throat chakra. However, it is okay to practice any of these exercises whenever you feel inclined to do so.

THROAT CHAKRA MANTRA: HAM

The Bija or seed mantra for the throat chakra is HAM.

HOW TO PRACTICE

1. In a seated or standing position, focus your mind's attention on the location of the throat chakra. (In the spine, just behind the throat.) Close your eyes and visualize a vibrant blue light glowing at this center.

2. Inhale to the count of six, and as you do so, imagine that the blue sphere of light is increasing in size.

3. Hold your breath until the count of three. While you do so, maintain the visualization of the blue ball of light radiating in the throat.

4. Exhale, and as you do so, chant HAM (as in hum). Visualize the light becoming smaller and finally being absorbed into this energy center. With your attention still focused on the throat chakra, rest here for a six count and repeat this exercise six to twelve times.

5. If the breathing counts are too long or short for you, feel free to adjust to accommodate your lung capacity. Do not hold your breath for extreme periods of time, as you may cause damage to your lungs, heart, or brain. As a rule of thumb, the length of time you hold your breath can be twice, or half, the length of your inhale.

TIP: If you inhale to the count of six, hold the breath for a three count.Or if you inhale to the count of six, hold the breath to the count of twelve. I do not recommend holding the breath for more than thirty seconds. Be smart! Be safe!

THROAT CHAKRA MUDRA

AKASH MUDRA

Akash Mudra, sometimes referred to as Shuni Mudra, will help stimulate, activate, and remove blockages from the throat center. In Sanskrit, Akash, or Akasha refers to the element of ether. Of the five fundamental elements in creation, the Akash element is considered to be the most powerful as it is the source of the other four elements. The Akasha Mudra balances the ether element and brings tranquility and alertness to the mind. It also enhances our communication abilities and helps cure a number of physical ailments.

HOW TO PRACTICE

To perform this mudra, sit in any position with your palms facing upward on your thighs. Bring together the tips of the thumb and middle finger and let them touch slightly without any force or tension. Allow the remaining three fingers to be stretched out straight, and rest your hands on your knees or thighs. Hold this mudra while also practicing the following pranayama exercise.

THROAT CHAKRA PRANAYAMA EXERCISE

1. While performing Akash Mudra, bring yourself to a comfortable seated position. Focus your mind's attention on the location of the throat chakra. (In the spine, just behind the throat.) Throw the breath out in a double exhalation, "Huh-huh."

2. Inhale deeply and fill the throat chakra with prana.

3. Without holding the breath, exhale completely and allow this energy to flow from the throat chakra and back down to the base of your spine.

4. As you come to the end of the exhale, mentally or verbally say, "I speak life into me."

5. Allow a brief pause, inhale, and repeat this exercise for sixteen minutes.

TIP: As you perform this exercise, you may change the word "life" to any other word that corresponds with your desires and wishes. For example, you may want to say, "I speak love into me" or "I speak peace and prosperity into me." Feel free to summon and express whatever energy your life calls for at this moment.

THROAT CHAKRA CRYSTALS

The following is a list of crystals you may use to help stimulate the throat chakra. These crystals may be worn as jewelry, kept in your purse or pocket, or placed on your desk or yoga mat during practice. You can even place them in your bathtub as you soak and take a nice relaxing bath. There are no hard rules as to when and how you can use crystals; just have fun including them in your practice.

Aquamarine:

Encourages truthfulness; heals emotional trauma; dissolves anger; brings calmness, peace, and tranquility of mind; calms the heart; helps one get in touch with buried or suppressed emotions

Sodalite:

Heals headaches; helpful against panic attacks, fevers, and anxiety; heals vocal cords; helps overcome writer's block; cleanses aura; releases old conditioning and programing; promotes calmness, self-confidence, and harmony; eases insomnia; stimulates the pineal gland; activates willpower, imagination, creativity, intuition, and self-assurance

Angelite:

Raises vibration; helps contact spirit guides and angels; helps connect with higher Self; enhances psychic abilities, telepathic communication, and enables astral travel; provides protection; heals headaches and infectious diseases.

Lapis Lazuli:

Soothes throat; strengthens neck; relieves insomnia; beneficial for singers, lecturers, speakers, and vocal performers; encourages integrity, leadership, intellect, and wisdom; awakens intuition; clears karma; stimulates psychic powers, insight, creative expression, and spiritual development

Blue Kyanite:

Heals back problems; natural pain reliever; promotes telepathy; helps ground spiritual energy and develop intuition; restores energy; aids in meditation; aligns all chakras; stimulates lucid dreaming, astral projection, and intuition; protects and purifies the astral body

Azurite:

Detoxifies the body; heals teeth, skin, bones, arthritis, joint problems, and throat problems; reduces stress, worry, depression, grief, and sadness; enhances spiritual connection; purifies home; clears tension and conflict; opens the mind to new perspectives; dissolves energy blockages; stimulates focus, clarity, empathy, compassion, channeling abilities, concentration, and communication abilities

THROAT CHAKRA AROMATHERAPY

The following is a list of essential oil, candle, or incense scents that you may use to stimulate and balance the throat chakra.

Frankincense	Basil	Juniper
Rosemary	Bergamot	Sandalwood
Eucalyptus	Chamomile	Peppermint
	Cypress	

THROAT CHAKRA JUICE

"ETHER"

Designed to stimulate and balance the throat chakra, this juice supports creative expression, healthy communication, and tranquility. The sweetness of *Ether* brings feelings of joy, confidence, and emotional ease, and it is guaranteed to lift your vibrations.

Ingredients

2 green apples	4–6 oz. of coconut	spirulina
2 kiwis	water	
½ cucumber	⅛ tbsp of blue	

DIRECTIONS

1. Working in this order, process the green apples, kiwis, and cucumber through a juicer according to the manufacturer's directions. (No juicer? See Tip.)

2. Add to juice 4–6 oz. of coconut water

3. Stir in ⅛ tbsp of blue spirulina and pour juice into a 16-oz. glass or mason jar

TIP: If you don't have a juicer, place the suggested amount of green apples, kiwis, and cucumber into your blender, and add 6–8 oz. of alkaline water. After blending, over a large bowl, pour the contents into a nut-milk bag. Squeeze the bag until all the liquid has been removed from the bag and only the fiber remains. Discard the fiber and pour 4–10 oz. of coconut water into the bowl. Finally, stir in ⅛ tbsp of blue spirulina and pour the juice from the bowl into a 16-oz. glass or mason jar. Shake well and enjoy!

Drink on an empty stomach to get the most benefits.

BENEFITS

Improves vision
Fights cancer
Cures headaches
Rich in protein
Hydrates the body
Anti-inflammatory

Improves heart health
Prevents diabetes
Detoxes heavy metals
Improves digestion

Lowers blood pressure
Boost energy and performance
Great for teeth, gums, and skin

THROAT CHAKRA FOODS

The following is a list of foods that help stimulate the throat chakra. Feel free to include them in your diet on the days in which you focus on this center.

VEGETABLES: Kale, spinach, arugula, broccoli, celery, bok choy, lettuce, collard greens, cucumbers, brussels sprouts

FRUITS: Avocadoes, green grapes, kiwis, pears, green apples, honeydew melons, limes

HERBS: Rosemary, thyme, sage, basil

TEA: Bayberry, Borage, Chamomile, Peppermint

THROAT CHAKRA AFFIRMATIONS

I am an expression of Divine calmness and peace.

I speak peace over my life.

I speak joy into my life.

I speak love over my life.

I speak success into my life.

I trust my inner voice.

I trust my highest self.

I live in truth. I speak truth.

I am honest, truthful, and sincere.

I express myself in a healthy way.

My words have the power to heal.

My words have the power to create.

I use my voice to heal others and create happiness.

I express my most authentic self.

I speak not to harm but to help.

I am aware of how my words impact others.

I choose them wisely. I express them lovingly.

I am not afraid to speak my mind.

I am not afraid to express my feelings.

I communicate with others in a healthy way.

I commune with myself in a healthy way.

I know how to listen.

I know how to accept constructive criticism.

I never take anyone or anything personally.

I am open to change.

I am open to improvement.

I accept change.

I accept improvement.

My potential is boundless. I express it.

My love is boundless. I express it.

My mind is boundless. I express it.

My life is boundless. I accept it.

I embrace and express beauty.

I embrace and express happiness.

I embrace and express my creative nature.

I embrace and express myself.

I am here to create.

I create daily.

I express my gifts. I celebrate my gifts. I share my gifts.

I speak love into the world.

I speak life into the world.

I want peace for all.

I want success for all.

I am living in the highest expression of love.

I am expressing the highest levels of peace.

I am everlasting love.

I am ever-increasing peace.

Pay attention to the advice that you lend to others. It is an opportunity to hear and adhere to the wisdom and truth of your own being.

POINTS OF DAILY INTROSPECTION

At the start of each day, the spiritual aspirant makes it a habit to practice impartial introspection. While viewing themselves with the soul's love and wisdom, inquire as to things that limit and suppress the expression of their highest nature. The following is a short list of introspective prompts that you may reflect upon during your morning meditation or journaling sessions.

- In what ways can I communicate who I am today?

- What do others say about the way I speak?

- Is this a fair representation of how I see myself?

- Do I feel heard by the people in my life?

- How can I ensure I am expressing myself effectively?

- How can I best serve others with my voice?

- Do I use my words to hurt or heal?

- What things are uncomfortable to talk about for me?

- How can I be even clearer when communicating?

POINTS OF NIGHTLY
INTROSPECTION

At the end of each day, the spiritual aspirant makes it a habit to impartially introspect on that day's activities. Nightly introspection allows one to see whether they made spiritual progress and remained committed to the tasks, goals, and intentions established at the start of the day. Writing these things in a spiritual diary allows us to clearly see our repetitive faults and our virtues and make adjustments wherever needed. The following is a short list of introspective prompts that you may reflect upon during or after your nightly meditation.

- What are some things I wish expressed or said today?

- How did holding on to these things affect my day?

- What are some things I shouldn't have said today?

- How did expressing these affect my day?

- Do I take the time to listen to my emotions for expressing them?

- In what ways can I improve how I express myself?

- Healing or hurt, what did I create with my words today?

- What do I need to communicate to myself at this moment?

EXPRESSING YOURSELF CAN ALSO LOOK LIKE:

- Singing
- Dancing
- Writing poetry
- Acting
- Cooking
- Doing photography
- Doing spoken word
- Acknowledging your emotions
- Saying how you feel
- Getting a new haircut or color
- Wearing something stylish
- Asking others how they want to be treated
- Letting others know how to love you
- Writing about your feelings
- Engaging in healthy conversations
- Hosting events
- Engaging with others online

Abundance is ever-present; you don't have to attract it. You only have to acknowledge it, be receptive, and accept your fair share of it.

SELF-CARE CHECK-IN

Sit briefly with the following questions; they will determine if you need to tune in and align with the balanced energy of the brow chakra.

- Do you want to be more discerning?

- Do you crave to know more about yourself?

- Do you want to develop your intuition?

- Do you find yourself being overly judgmental or critical of yourself and others?

- Do you find it hard to concentrate or meditate?

- Is your life out of focus with your vision?

- Do you feel aligned with your Highest Self?

- Do you trust your Higher Self?

- Do you feel imaginative?

- Is your soul happy with this experience?

After checking in with yourself, how satisfied are you with the answers you gave to the questions above? This is where the shift starts to happen, and you begin to consciously understand and master your energy. If your answers to the questions above were unsatisfactory to you, this is an indication to focus on the brow chakra today. You can find the Brow Chakra Sadhana in the following chapter. The practice should take you no more than an hour, but there are also auxiliary practices and exercises you may do to further balance the energy in the brow chakra. If you are working on this center, please try not to mix the practices from other chapters with it. The more focus you place on a particular center, the more that energy awakens, and the stronger it becomes. Become more acquainted with yourself today. Challenge yourself to go deeper into your practices and break free from the limits you have imposed upon yourself—set your soul free.

Watch yourself. Become aware of your behavior, your habits, your responses, and your reactions. You have the power to change them— if only you are aware.

KNOW YOURSELF:

BROW CHAKRA OVERVIEW

Knowledge is the nectar of the soul. Its sweetness awakens us from the slumber of self-forgetfulness and frees us from all suffering and sorrow. There is no greater bliss than knowledge, and when we endeavor to know ourselves, we embark on a journey that brings complete satisfaction and self-illumination. To know yourself is to love yourself. But who are you? You are not the body. You are not your possessions; You are not your profession; You are not even your personality. You are the changeless reality that allows the expression of all these things. The body will change and start to slowly decay over time. Your possessions, profession, and personality will all change during the course of your life. But you, the soul, the Self, will remain changeless amidst the ever changing.

The soul was made for self-knowledge and self-realization. You have no higher purpose in this life than to know the Self. What brings suffering? I say it is nothing more than the ignorance of Self. We suffer because we do not know who we are and what we are. Fear and worry plague our lives because we live in constant forgetfulness of the Self. We tend to identify more with the body. Though the human body may be beautiful, it is constantly giving us trouble, and in the end, it is thrown in the grave. The Self is fearless and free from worry because it knows that it cannot die, it cannot be burned, it cannot be cut, it cannot be hurt, broken, or buried. But what is this Self? The Self is the pure consciousness that is witnessing the changes of this cosmic play. The Self is the play, the players, and the act of playing.

The Self is all and in all. And all is in the Self. The primary thing you must know about yourself is, you are *That*. Your true identity is the luminous, eternal light of the soul. Remind yourself of this constantly, and the lotus of self-knowledge will bloom within you.

ALONG MY JOURNEY

In my journey into knowing myself, I have found a greater appreciation for life, people, animals, Nature, and all of creation. Most importantly, I have deepened my relationship with God. As an adolescent, being raised in a Christian community, for the most part, I was uninspired by the stories and depictions of the Bible. Not because I didn't believe them to be true, but because I wanted living proof. I wanted to experience the truth that Christ spoke for myself, not just read about it. I wanted to consciously express the peace, joy, love, and boundlessness of God. Not just hear beautiful sermons that often made me feel like these things could only be expressed by a chosen few. Not having the necessary resources or guidance to nurture my inquisitive nature growing up led me to gradually abandon religion in my life.

I've always been a practical person, and I wanted no part in something I could not be shown how to experience. Thankfully, after many struggles and seasons of darkness, I began to look within for the answers I sought without. Self-inquiry has led me to self-knowledge and the blossoming of peace, wisdom, joy, and love in the garden of my soul. Through self-knowledge, I have grown to know God as an intimate friend and beloved companion. I now realize that God is not separate from me, that God did not create me, but God has become me, and God has become all. Now, there is not a moment that goes by when I don't see or feel the presence of the ever-present One. Having found the god within me allows me to resonate with and commune with the god within everyone and everything. The disdain I had for religion growing up has been transmuted into a deep adoration and respect for those great souls, who, through self-knowledge, made themselves vessels of light. My own self-realization has granted me the vision to see the underlying unity of all paths—they lead to the One.

ABOUT THIS CHAKRA

The Sanskrit name for the brow chakra is Ajna. The word *Ajna* means "to perceive," "to command," or "beyond wisdom." Though the Ajna chakra is located in the medulla, just about where the spine meets the brain, it is reflected in the forehead between the eyebrows. For this reason, it is also known as the "Third Eye" or "brow chakra." The brow chakra is the seat of the soul, and it is symbolically represented by a lotus flower with two petals, which represent the sun and moon. The color associated with this chakra is indigo. It does not correlate to any of the senses or sense organs and is beyond all elements (though it is often said to be associated with light). The Ajna chakra is sometimes called the jnana chakra (knowledge chakra) or ajnana chakra (ignorance chakra). Within and above this center is the place of knowledge, and below the center is the play of ignorance. Ordinary, our consciousness flows downward toward the lower chakras, which keep us engaged in the world of matter. But when the consciousness is concentrated on and lifted up to this center, we free ourselves from the world illusion and enter the Kingdom of Spirit.

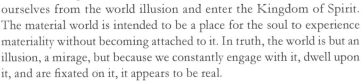

The material world is intended to be a place for the soul to experience materiality without becoming attached to it. In truth, the world is but an illusion, a mirage, but because we constantly engage with it, dwell upon it, and are fixated on it, it appears to be real.

The dream of the world is dissolved in the Ajna chakra. In the spiritual center of the third eye, we see the entire cosmic play as a massive show of light. The spiritual seeker who concentrates and meditates upon the Ajna chakra is blessed with the vision to "see" beyond the illusion of matter and perceive the glory of spirit within and beyond creation. Generally, we all have two eyes, the eyes of duality, in which we perceive good and bad, right and wrong, friends and foes, pain and pleasure. This perceived duality is the cause of bondage, ignorance, and suffering. When the third eye chakra is activated and opened by consistent and deep meditation, the ignorance of duality is dissolved, and we see the world with a single eye. Harmony, unity, and oneness amidst the apparent duality of the world are thus cultivated.

The third eye, also known as the "Christ Center," is the single eye that Christ spoke of when he said, "The light of the body is within the eye, if therefore thine eye be single, thy whole body shall be full of light." Light is wisdom, purity, understanding, and knowledge. With the awakening of the brow chakra, our knowledge and understanding of both the inner and outer worlds gradually expand, and we awaken to the true nature and purity of our being. Though we experience darkness or ignorance while living in the material realm, light is what we are. We are the knowledge and wisdom of the soul, and we are the all-powerful consciousness that pervades every atom and particle in the universe. Realize that you are the universe, the cosmos, and everything in it. Knowledge of Self brings forth this realization.

The brow chakra is the key to unlocking the secrets of the soul and the universe. As we evolve spiritually and develop this center, our inner eye is awakened, and we not only see our true selves, but we also understand what we see with profound truth and knowledge. The brow chakra, when activated, grants us powers such as clairvoyance, mental equanimity, discernment, control over adverse situations, and supreme control over the lower nature.

SIGNS OF BALANCE AND IMBALANCE

When your brow chakra is open or balanced, you may experience or feel the following:

- Inner peace
- Inner love
- Attentiveness
- Imaginative

- Discernment
- Clairvoyance
- Open-mindedness
- Extreme calmness

- Heightened intuition
- Complete self-control

When your brow chakra is blocked or imbalanced, you may experience or feel the following:

- Anxiety
- Insomnia
- Depression
- Hallucinations

- Fear
- Poor judgment
- Paranoia
- Extreme skepticism

- Difficulty concentrating

Physical signs and symptoms of imbalances in the brow chakra may also include:

- Migraines
- Sinusitis

- Seizures
- Poor vision

- Sciatica

BROW CHAKRA SADHANA

AFFIRMATION

"I see myself as a radiant light of love, peace, and wisdom. I know myself to be a reflection of all that I see."

MEDITATION

Listen to the "Know Yourself: Brow Chakra Meditation."

Available on streaming apps and YouTube.

EXERCISE

Notice your immediate surroundings and the things that you see. In what ways do they describe who you are? Can you see yourself in these things? Spend a few moments reflecting, and journal your thoughts.

POSE OF THE DAY

UTTANASANA
(STANDING FORWARD FOLD)

Yoga postures that involve forward folds and inversions are perfect for stimulating the brow chakra. These postures allow the prana latent blood to flow to the face and head area, which leads to the stimulation of this center. Uttanasana, or standing forward fold, is a simple but effective asana that will **help energize the eye chakra**. Like all forward folds, Uttanasana helps bring balance, clarity, and equanimity to the mind. This asana is also said to relieve stress and increase patience.

BENEFITS

Calms the mind	Stimulates the liver and kidneys	issues
Reduces fatigue		Improves hip mobility
Relieves headaches	Heals digestive	

UTTANASANA (STANDING FORWARD FOLD)

1. Stand with your feet together on your mat. Bend your knees slightly and fold your torso over your legs.

2. Keep your hips stationary and continue to bend forward comfortably.

3. Place your hands next to your feet or on the ground. (You may also grab your ankles, or shins if your body won't allow you to touch the floor.)

4. Inhale to expand your chest and lengthen your spine.

5. Exhale and gently press both legs straight without locking your knees.

6. Keep your neck long and the crown of your head facing toward the ground.

7. Inhale and lift out of this position by, softening your knees, hinging up at your hips, and lifting your spine one vertebrae at a time.

8. Try repeating this three to six times to get the full benefits of this pose. If you are at home and on your yoga mat, feel free to flow into any other asanas that complement today's practice. Listen to your body and gently flow into whatever feels natural and appropriate for today's practice.

Asanas that balance the brow chakra:

Child's Pose (Balasana)

Locust Pose (Salabhasana)

Extended Puppy Pose (Uttana Shishosana)

Downward-Facing Dog (Adho Mukha Svanasana)

Pyramid Pose (Parsvottanasana)

Standing Forward Fold (Uttanasana)

Dolphin Pose, (Ardha Pincha

Mayurasana)

Head-to-Knee Pose (Janu Sirsasana)

Legs Up the Wall Pose (Viparita Karani)

Knees to Chest Pose (Apanasana)

REMINDER

Be mindful of how you see yourself. Being overly judgmental, analytical, and hypercritical of ourselves causes us to doubt and lose confidence in who we are. We always strive to see ourselves with eyes of compassion, mercy, and understanding. Know that you are an ever-blossoming flower of light and love. The universe itself is ever expanding and eternal. The universe within you is also of this nature. Never think that you are done growing, learning, or evolving spiritually. But also, never condemn yourself for being where you are currently. Getting to know yourself is a lifelong journey, and if you take your time, you will grow faster. Be patient with yourself and your spiritual journey. The fruits of your spiritual endeavors are subtle and are not always easily forthcoming.

Don't allow yourself to be discouraged if you fail to see outer or inner results. A flower blooms according to the season, not overnight. Allow the flower of the spiritual journey to unfold naturally as you water and nurture the seed of your soul. Ceaselessly inquire about the nature of your being, the nature of the universe, and the source of it. The Spirit adores and supports those who question and ponder the mysteries of the soul. Always be seeking to know more about yourself. Through self-study and introspection, you will, without fail, attain the bliss of that supreme knowledge. The Self is all-satisfying, and to those who have become acquainted with it, they find inner and outer fulfillment—in this world and beyond.

BROW CHAKRA AUXILIARY PRACTICES

In this section, you will find additional exercises, tips, and readings that can be implemented in today's routine. The exercises can be done in any particular order, at any point in time during the day. To stay in alignment with the theme of this section, it is best to practice these exercises on the days that you have chosen to focus on your throat chakra. However, it is okay to practice any of these exercises whenever you feel inclined to do so.

BROW CHAKRA MANTRA: OM

The Bija or seed mantra for the brow chakra is OM.

HOW TO PRACTICE

1. In a seated or standing position, focus your mind's attention on the location of the brow chakra. (In the forehead, just between the eyebrows.) Close your eyes and visualize a vibrant dark blue light glowing at this center.

2. Inhale to the count of six, and as you do so, imagine that the dark blue ball of light is increasing in size.

3. Hold your breath until the count of three. While you do so, maintain the visualization of the dark blue ball of light radiating in the third eye.

4. Exhale, and as you do so, chant OM (OM as in omni). Visualize the light becoming smaller and finally being absorbed into this energy center. With your attention still focused on the brow chakra, rest here for six seconds and repeat this exercise two more times.

5. If the breathing counts are too long or short for you, feel free to adjust to accommodate your lung capacity. Do not hold your breath for extreme periods of time, as you may cause damage to your lungs, heart, or brain. As a rule of thumb, the length of time you hold your breath can be twice, or half, the length of your inhale.

BROW CHAKRA MUDRA

KALESVARA MUDRA

Kalesvara Mudra is a gesture that will help bring stimulation and activation to the Ajna, or brow chakra. When practiced, this mudra opens energy channels in the brain, which bring extreme calmness and concentration to the mind. Kalesvara Mudra also enhances memory, improves our introspective power, and aids in removing unwanted character traits and behaviors.

HOW TO PRACTICE

To perform this mudra, bring both hands together to form the shape of a heart. With the tips of the thumbs touching, lift up both middle fingers and allow their tips to touch. Holding this mudra, place your hands in your lap while meditating or practicing the following pranayama exercise.

BROW CHAKRA PRANAYAMA EXERCISE

1. While performing Kalesvara Mudra, bring yourself to a comfortable seated position. Focus your mind's attention on the brow chakra or third eye. (In the forehead, just between the eyebrows.) Throw the breath out in a double exhalation, "Huh-huh."

2. Inhale completely and imagine a dark blue sphere of light rising from the base of your spine up to the third eye.

3. With your attention focused on the third eye, hold the breath here for a three count and then exhale completely, allowing the breath to flow back down to the base of your spine.

4. As you come to the end of the exhale, mentally or verbally say, "I am light."

5. Allow a brief pause, inhale, and repeat this exercise for twelve minutes.

If you're thinking too much. You're not breathing enough.

BROW CHAKRA CRYSTALS

The following is a list of crystals you may use to help stimulate the brow chakra. These crystals may be worn as jewelry, kept in your purse or pocket, or placed on your desk or yoga mat during practice. You can even place them in your bathtub as you soak and take a nice relaxing bath. There are no hard rules as to when and how you can use crystals; just have fun including them in your practice.

Iolite:

Harmonizes emotions; dissolves fear; helps one stay in the moment; enhances spiritual growth; aids in introspection; helps attract spirit guides; encourages wisdom, happiness, discernment, peace, balance, exploration, and calmness; aids in astral travel; enhances psychic abilities

Unakite:

Muscle relaxer; helps hair growth; aids in tissue repair; aids in healthy pregnancy; releases emotional blockages; encourages self-love and compassion; reduces sorrow, grief, and pity; protects against low vibrations; purifies the environment; protects plants from disease

Amethyst:

Aids in healing body ailments and sickness; removes addictions; clears aura; offers astral travel protection; facilitates clear connection with the Divine; transmutes low vibrations to higher vibrations; awakens intuition

Clear Quartz:

Helps unlock memory; clears auras; can be programed for anything; aligns subtle bodies; cleanses and clears crystals; energizes crystals, plants, and body; brings harmony, clairvoyance, and chakra alignment

Labradorite:

Lowers metabolism; inspires creativity; relieves insecurities; brings clarity to meditation; promotes enthusiasm, self-confidence, and discernment; stimulates transformation, imagination, and lucid dreaming

Herkimer Diamond:

Reduces pain; clears the body of toxins; brings inner understanding; aids in introspection; helps heal the emotional body; helps remove fear and trapped emotions; purifies the energy field; helps one send and receive positive vibrations

BROW CHAKRA AROMATHERAPY

The following is a list of essential oil, candle, or incense scents that you may use to stimulate and balance the brow chakra.

Pure Angelica

Bay laurel

Clary sage

Cypress

Juniper

Sweet marjoram

Sandalwood

BROW CHAKRA JUICE

"LIQUID AMETHYST"

Designed to support and balance the brow chakra, this juice brings focus, calmness, and mental alertness to the mind and a sense of ease and rejuvenation to the body. *Liquid Amethyst* also stimulates the third eye and makes you feel in harmony within yourself and your surroundings.

Ingredients

5 cups of blueberries	1 inch of ginger	⅛ tbsp of butterfly
1 celery stalk	8–10 oz. of coconut water	pea powder

DIRECTIONS

1. Working in this order, process blueberries, celery, and ginger through a juicer according to the manufacturer's directions. (No juicer? See Tip.)

2. Add to juice 8–10 oz. of coconut water

3. Stir in ⅛ tbsp of butterfly pea powder and pour juice into a 16-oz. glass or mason jar

TIP: If you don't have a juicer, place the suggested amount of blueberries, celery, and ginger into your blender, and add 4–6 oz. of alkaline water. After blending, over a large bowl, pour the contents into a nut-milk bag. Squeeze the bag until all the liquid has been removed from the bag and only the fiber remains. Discard the fiber and pour 8–10 oz. of coconut water into the bowl. Finally, stir in 1/8 tbsp of butterfly pea powder and pour the juice from the bowl into a 16-oz. glass or mason jar. Shake well and enjoy!

Drink on an empty stomach to get the most benefits.

BENEFITS

Antioxidants
Anti-inflammatory
Antidepressant
Boosts metabolism
Improves eyesight

Immune booster
Boosts brain health
Improves memory
Improves digestion
Supports healthy skin

Improves mental health
Helps with hair growth

BROW CHAKRA FOODS

The list below contains a list of foods that help stimulate the brow chakra. Feel free to include them in your diet on the days in which you focus on this center.

VEGETABLES: Purple cabbage, purple kale, purple-fleshed potatoes, purple carrots, purple asparagus, purple peppers, purple kohlrabi, eggplant

FRUITS: Elderberries, boysenberries, black currants, purple grapes, figs, plums

HERBS: Ginkgo, lavender, sage, mugwort, cinquefoil, lobelia, roses, copal

TEA: White tea, elderflower, blueberry, eyebright

BROW CHAKRA AFFIRMATIONS

I know that my life is in Divine care.

I trust the inner light that guides me.

My heart is expanding.

My consciousness is expanding.

I see beauty and love everywhere that I go.

I feel beauty and love in everyone that I see.

I see Divine light.

I am Divine light.

I see God in all.

I am God in all.

My life is not separate from life.

The entire universe is my body.

When I hurt others, I also hurt myself.

When I help others, I also help myself.

When I condemn others, I also condemn myself.

When I celebrate others, I also celebrate myself.

All is my Self. I embrace myself in all.

I accept myself in all.

I see life with a single eye and an equal mind.

Everything is okay. Everything is all right.

I will do my best to bring love and light into this dimension.

I am conscious love. I am conscious light.

I am eternal energy. I am eternal light.

I use my mind to create my reality.

My mind is full of positive and creative thoughts.

I reject thoughts that do not fit into my world of peace.

I reject thoughts that do not agree with my world of love.

I am the creator of my reality.

I am the master of my destiny.

I am connected with Source at all times.

I am connected with Source at all times.

I am one with Source at all times.

I am an expression of Source.

I am Source Energy expressing itself.

I am connected to all. I am all.

I am absolute oneness.

I am omnipresent unity.

I am OM.
I am OM.
I am OM.

Shadow work is light work. Keep moving through the darkness and lovingly offer illumination to all parts of you.

POINTS OF DAILY INTROSPECTION

At the start of each day, the spiritual aspirant makes it a habit to practice impartial introspection. While viewing themselves with the soul's love and wisdom, inquire as to things that limit and suppress the expression of their highest nature. The following is a short list of introspective prompts that you may reflect upon during your morning meditation or journaling sessions.

- How do I see myself?

- Is this based upon my perception or the views of others?

- How do others see me?

- Is this who I think I am and project myself to be?

- What does it mean to know myself?

- How much time will I dedicate to knowing myself?

- What activities help me understand and know myself?

- If my life was a movie, what would be the title?

- What actress or actor would play me?

POINTS OF NIGHTLY INTROSPECTION

At the end of each day, the spiritual aspirant makes it a habit to impartially introspect on that day's activities. Nightly introspection allows one to see whether they made spiritual progress and remained committed to the tasks, goals, and intentions established at the start of the day. Writing these things in a spiritual diary allows us to clearly see our repetitive faults and our virtues and make adjustments wherever needed. The following is a short list of introspective prompts that you may reflect upon during or after your nightly meditation.

- How often do I remember my divinity?

- What helped me get a better understanding of myself today?

- Did I lose sight of my true Self and nature today?

- What caused my forgetfulness?

- How can I remember who I am?

- Am I satisfied with how much I understand myself?

- How do my relationships convey who I am?

- Do I see a connection between myself and others?

- Who do I want to get to know and why?

KNOWING YOURSELF
CAN ALSO LOOK LIKE:

- Journaling
- Introspecting
- Meditating
- Practicing asanas
- Doing shadow work
- Chanting mantras
- Spending time in Nature
- Reading spiritual books

- Enjoying silence and solitude
- Consciously breathing
- Fasting
- Self-inquiring
- Studying scriptures
- Keeping good company

Ritualize rest and solitude. Come back to you in celebration.

SELF-CARE CHECK-IN

Sit briefly with the following questions; they will determine if you need to tune in and align with the balanced energy of the crown chakra.

- Do you need to rest?

- Are you uncomfortable with doing nothing?

- Do you feel disconnected from you?

- Do you feel connected to Source and Source energy?

- Do you find it hard to be yourself around others?

- Are you lacking clarity at the moment?

- Do you worry about things that are out of your control?

- Do you feel that you are in control?

- Do you feel worthy?

- Do you feel overworked or exhausted?

- Do you need to disconnect from the world socially?

After checking in with yourself, how satisfied are you with the answers you gave to the questions above? This is where the shift starts to happen, and you begin to consciously understand and master your energy. If your answers to the questions above were unsatisfactory to you, this is an indication to focus on the crown chakra today. You can find the Crown Chakra Sadhana in the following chapter. The practice should take you no more than an hour, but there are also auxiliary practices and exercises you may do to further balance the energy in the crown chakra. If you are working on this energy, please try not to mix the practices from other chapters with it. The more focus you place on a particular center, the more that energy awakens, and the stronger it becomes. Get comfortable with being you—it's all you can ever be.

Being yourself is your superpower.

BE YOURSELF:
CROWN CHAKRA
OVERVIEW

The most beautiful thing you can be is yourself. There is no one like you, and for the rest of eternity, there will never be another quite like you. Everything that makes you different, awkward, or strange is everything that makes you unforgettably you. No one can be or replace you, and that is your gift to the world. Through your own eyes, you paint a unique picture of the world in which we all live. You notice beauty in hidden places. You appreciate things that go unseen. You see colors and hues illustrated on the canvas of creation in ways that others could never imagine them. You speak and sing about things that life would not dare to whisper to another. You are a unique channel in which the infinite cosmos expresses and offers a new perspective to the world. You are not a mistake; you are a miracle.

Accept and trust that you are enough as you are. There is nothing that you lack, and there is nothing to become. You have come from the infinite source of wisdom, love, beauty, and abundance. And all that it is, you are. Have the confidence and courage to be exactly who you are today without the need to compare yourself or your life to others. Comparison kills confidence and makes us feel as though we are less than what we are. When we compare our lives, we dim our light and fail to acknowledge the profound uniqueness of it. You have to try to be like others, but you don't have to try to be yourself. It happens naturally the more you let go of comparison and all the ideas of perfection you have in your mind. Be secure and celebrate your individuality. Embrace and honor your personality. To be perfectly you is perfectly okay.

ALONG MY JOURNEY

The spiritual journey has taught me so much about being and showing up as the person I am today. No more do I find the urge or intense desire to be anything other than who I am at this moment. At this moment, I know that I am perfect, whole, complete, and enough. I know that there is nothing to become, for in trying to become, I lose sight of all that I am now. Yes, I still have ambitions and goals, but no longer are they seen as something to be obtained outside of myself. I know that whatever I desire is within me, and if I am willing to align with that which is within me, life will present these things to me. Like many of us, I was taught from an early age that I had to become something, that I had to go out and get the things I wanted in life. But along this new path, I have found beauty in unbecoming. Day by day, I find joy in shedding layers, removing fears, doubts, worries, and unhealthy beliefs. Becoming totally empty. That is where I now find fulfillment. In being nothing. Desiring nothing. Needing nothing. Pouring out everything and becoming nobody. Forgetting the world of things. Melting away the fabric of time and space. Dissolving into pure nothingness. In that nothingness, I have found everything. I have found me. Pure being.

ABOUT THIS CHAKRA

The Sanskrit name for the crown chakra is Sahasrara, which literally means "thousand petaled." This center is also known as "Brahmarandhra" (the door of the Infinite). The Sahasrara chakra is located at the crown or top of the head. As its name suggests, the Sahasrara chakra is symbolically represented by a lotus flower with a thousand petals. No colors or qualities are associated with this center because it represents the domain of Spirit, which is beyond names, forms, and description. "The Kingdom of God is within you," and the crown chakra is that Divine palace in which the consciousness of the infinite reigns. One who meditates upon and lifts their consciousness up to this center not only reflects but embodies Cosmic Consciousness. But this chakra is awakened and opened only through Divine grace and surrender. Though we may chant mantras, perform austerities, study scriptures, and practice our sadhana perfectly, it is only through Divine Grace that we enter into the kingdom of Cosmic Consciousness. The crown chakra is the seat of wisdom and enlightenment. One whose soul has merged with Spirit in the crown center is saturated with Divine bliss, supreme knowledge, and purity of being. No longer bound by the mind, body, and world of matter, they free themselves from the cycles of birth and rebirth and attain final liberation.

SIGNS OF BALANCE AND IMBALANCE

When your crown chakra is open or balanced, you may experience or feel the following:

Blissful

Intuitive

Harmonious

Dispassionate

Divinely connected

When your crown chakra is blocked or imbalanced, you may experience or feel the following:

Confusion

Uninspired

Poor memory

Judgmental

Overly analytical

Superiority complex

Desire to oversleep

Light sensitivity

Disconnected from Source

Physical signs and symptoms of imbalances in the crown chakra may also include:

Exhaustion

Chronic headaches

Poor coordination

CROWN CHAKRA
SADHANA

AFFIRMATION

"There is a time for rest and a time for activity.
In relaxation and stillness, I am recharged and renewed."

MEDITATION

Listen to the "Be Yourself: Crown Chakra Meditation."
Available on streaming apps and YouTube.

EXERCISE

Rest, relax, and do absolutely nothing today.
Allow yourself to simply be.

POSE OF THE DAY

SAVASANA (CORPSE POSE)

Total rest and relaxation are a dreading challenge for most of us living in this fast-paced, always-on-the-go society we have grown accustomed to. It is for this reason that Savasana or corpse pose, which appears to be easy, is perhaps the most difficult posture for yoga practitioners. Although the physical challenges of twists, turns, bends, inversions, and balancing acts performed in other yoga poses require great strength and fortitude, they do not challenge us quite like Savasana. Relaxation does not happen through any forceful action or command. It happens by allowing ourselves to simply be. In Savasana, we grow to understand the subtle power and rejuvenation that rest and relaxation bring. Becoming totally relaxed and empty of any will to move or hold on to the body, we are thus filled with fresh new life and cosmic energy.

BENEFITS

Calms the mind	Brings total relaxation	fatigue
Reduces anxiety		Reduces high blood pressure
Improves sleep	Reduces stress and	

HOW TO DO SAVASANA (CORPSE POSE)

1. Lying on your back, place your arms down by your side and let your feet drop open.

2. Close your eyes, take a few deep, slow breaths and allow your body to soften and become more relaxed as you breathe.

3. Mentally scan the body from the crown of your head to your toes, noticing any tightness or restlessness.

4. With every exhale, send a wave of relaxation to these areas.

5. Forget the breath, let go of your body, and allow your mind to rest completely in stillness.

6. Stay in Savasana for 5–15 minutes

7. To exit this pose, slowly deepen the breath and bring a little movement to your body by wiggling your toes and fingers.

8. Bring your hands over your head and roll over to either side of your body. Bring your knees to check and curl up into a fetal position.

9. When you are ready, gently lift yourself up into a seated position and stay here for as long as you like.

Asanas that balance the crown chakra:

Crocodile Pose
(Makarasana

Rabbit Stand
(Sasangasana)

Dolphin Pose
(Ardha Pincha
Mayurasana)

Half Camel Pose
(Ardha Ustrasana)

Headstand
(Sirasana)

Tree Pose
(Vrksasana)

Standing Prayer
Backbend
(Anuvittasana)

Corpse Pose
(Savasana)

REMINDER

It's okay to be empty. Empty of worry. Empty of fear. Empty of all that keeps the soul captive and enslaved. Pour out everything and allow yourself to be completely empty. Society has so conditioned us to believe that we have to become something, that we have to always be in a state of constant chase, gain, and accusation. We don't realize how much suffering and self-inflicted sorrow we induce upon ourselves by living a life of constant chase. Rarely are we satisfied with what we have or where we are in our lives. There is always a constant urge to add bigger, better, and larger things to our bounty. This is understandable because we are boundless and infinite beings, and as such, we want to express the infinite nature of the soul on the material plane. But it is also one of our biggest flaws because no gain in the world can quite satisfy or appease the mind.

The mind is always in constant chase and in search of something that will be greater than the abundance of the soul. But to no avail, it can never gather enough things to eclipse the all-satisfying joy of the soul. One of the greatest spiritual virtues is contentment. One who is content is satisfied in the self. And because the Self is all-knowing and abundant in nature, it fulfills the individual's immediate needs without fail. To chase or hanker after anything is to denounce and ignore the abundant power of the soul. You are the soul. You are and will always be more than enough. When you realize your true worth, all that you chased will chase you.

CROWN CHAKRA
AUXILIARY PRACTICES

In this section, you will find additional exercises, tips, and readings that can be implemented in today's routine. The exercises can be done in any particular order, at any point in time during the day. To stay in alignment with the theme of this section, it is best to practice these exercises on the days that you have chosen to focus on your crown chakra. However, it is okay to practice any of these exercises whenever you feel inclined to do so.

CROWN CHAKRA MANTRA: N/A

There is no Bija or seed mantra for the crown chakra. When concentrating on this center, observe silence and listen for the sound of the OM vibration.

ABOUT THE OM VIBRATION.

The Om vibration is considered to be the sound of the universe and the mother of all sounds. All things contain and are contained in the OM vibration. All things, animate and inanimate, vibrate the sacred sound of OM. When there was nothing in the universe, no stars, no planets, no atoms, and no particles of matter, there was OM. "The intelligent cosmic energy of OM that issues forth from Cosmic Consciousness, and is the manifestation of God, is the Creator and substance of all matter. This sacred vibration is the link between matter and Spirit. Meditation on OM is the way to realize the true Spirit-essence of all creation. By inwardly following the sound of OM to its source, the consciousness is carried aloft to God or God Consciousness.

"As the spiritual aspirant concentrates on OM, first by mentally chanting Aum, and then by actually hearing that sound, the mind is diverted from the physical sounds of matter outside the body to the other sounds of the vibrating flesh. Then the consciousness is diverted from the vibrations of the physical body to the musical vibrations of the chakras in the astral body. When the aspirant's consciousness is able not only to hear the cosmic sound of OM, but also to feel its actual presence in every unit of space, in all finite vibrating matter, then the soul of that individual becomes one with the Om vibration." (Paramahansa Yogananda)

HOW TO PRACTICE

1. In a seated position, focus your mind's attention on the location of the Third Eye or the crown chakra (at the top of the head). Visualize a vibrant purple light glowing at this center.

2. Inhale deeply, exhale completely, then allow the breath to flow in and out naturally on its own.

3. Place both thumbs over both ears and rest the other fingers on your scalp. Listen intently for any audible sounds that may emit from the chakras. If you should hear any sound, focus your attention on it completely. If you fail to hear any sounds, that's okay. With continued practice, you will develop the ability to hear the OM vibration.

SOUNDS OF THE CHAKRAS

Each chakra emits a particular sound that can be heard while in meditation. The Muladhara or root chakra emits a sound that is similar to that of a swarm of buzzing bees. The Swadhistana or sacral center vibrates the sound similar to that of a flute. The Manipuri or solar plexus vibrates the sound similar to that of a harp. The Anāhata or heart chakra vibrates the sound similar to that of bells. The Vishuddha or throat chakra vibrates a sound that is similar to the roar of an ocean. The Anja or brow chakra vibrates the sound of OM, which sounds like a chorus of all these sounds combined.

This practice should be done after meditation periods. If you fail to hear any sounds, don't be discouraged; continue to make every day's meditation deeper than the last. The more you practice deep meditation, these sounds will naturally become a part of your experience.

CROWN CHAKRA MUDRA

ADI MUDRA

Adi Mudra comes from the Sanskrit root word *adi*, which means "first or primal" and *mudra* meaning "gesture or seal." Adi mudra is called the "first mudra" because it is the first position the hands of the fetus are capable of making inside the womb of the mother. This mudra helps calm the mind, increase lung capacity, stimulate oxygen flow to the head, and quiet the nervous system.

HOW TO PRACTICE

To perform this mudra, sit in any position with your palms facing upward on your thighs. Bring the tip of your thumb to meet the base of your pinky, and curl the other four fingers over the thumb. Turn your hands over so that your palms are facing downward and resting on your thighs or knees.

BE YOURSELF: CROWN CHAKRA

CROWN CHAKRA PRANAYAMA EXERCISE

While sitting in a comfortable position and performing Adi Mudra, focus your mind's attention on the location of the base of your spine. Throw the breath out in a double exhalation, "Huh-huh."

Inhale deeply and slowly until the count of four, bringing the breath up from the base of your spine to your crown chakra.

With your attention focused on the crown center, hold the breath here until the count of three.

Exhale until the count of six, and at the end of the exhale, keep the breath out until the count of three.

Inhale and repeat this breathing exercise seven times.

True success is happiness. True happiness is never more than a breath away.

CROWN CHAKRA CRYSTALS

The following is a list of crystals you may use to help stimulate the crown chakra. These crystals may be worn as jewelry, kept in your purse or pocket, or placed on your desk or yoga mat during practice. You can even place them in your bathtub as you soak and take a nice relaxing bath. There are no hard rules as to when and how you can use crystals; just have fun including them in your practice.

Sugilite

Boosts the immune system; helps regenerate cellular structure; heightens spiritual awareness; protects empaths; promotes harmony and universal love; heals trauma and protects energy; stimulates kundalini; encourages self-love, peace of mind, self-empowerment, and spiritual growth

Selenite:

Heals physical and etheric bodies; use for good luck and protection; evokes angels; protects from harmful energies; clears, opens, and activates the crown chakra; helps explore past lives; aids in spiritual growth; strengthens telepathy; stimulates clairvoyance and clairaudience

Charoite:

Heals liver issues; cures insomnia; soothes headaches; detoxifies the body; raises vibration; helps release mental and emotional attachments; inspires courage; lifts self-esteem; activates patience, forgiveness, unconditional love, contentment, and psychic abilities

Lepidolite:

Brings emotional healing; reduces stress and anxiety; helps deepens meditation; helps improve sleep; encourages independence

Indigo Gabbro:

Helps raise vibration; develops intuition and psychic abilities; helps connect with higher Self; brings spiritual grounding—aids in shadow work

Rutilated Quartz:

Heals emotional wounds and trauma; antidepressant; cleanses and recharges all chakras; magnifies goals and dreams; aids in self-realization and transformation

Howlite:

Strengthens bones and teeth; balances calcium levels; relieves and can even eliminate stress; helps one gain insight into past lives; helps overcome critical behavior; sharpens memory; improves sleep; strengthens meditation; promotes relaxation, patience, calmness, and concentration

CROWN CHAKRA AROMATHERAPY

The following is a list of essential oils that you may use to stimulate and balance the crown chakra.

Cedarwood	Galbanum	Jasmine
Elemi	Gurjum	Lavender
Frankincense	Helichrysum	

CROWN CHAKRA JUICE

"SAMADHI"

Designed to balance the crown chakra, this juice stimulates relaxation and pure bliss. It provides support for those who may be on a liquid fast by helping curve cravings and brings necessary energy to the body. *Samadhi* induces feelings of peace, joy, and inner satisfaction.

Ingredients

2 dragon fruit
8 oz. of coconut water

½ lemon
1 tbsp agave

DIRECTIONS

1. Working in this order, process the peeled dragon fruit through a juicer according to the manufacturer's directions. (No juicer? See Tip.)

2. Add 8 oz. of coconut water

3. Add to juice 10 ml of freshly squeezed lemon juice (the equivalent of ½ lemon)

4. Stir in 1 tbsp of agave and pour juice into a 16-oz. glass or mason jar

TIP: If you don't have a juicer, place the suggested amount of peeled dragon fruit into your blender, and add 4–6 oz. of alkaline water. After blending, over a large bowl, pour the contents into a nut-milk bag. Squeeze the bag until all the liquid has been removed from the bag and only the fiber remains. Discard the fiber and pour into the bowl 8 oz. of coconut water. Next, add 10 ml of freshly squeezed lemon juice (The equivalent of ½ lemon), and stir in 1 tbsp of agave. Finally, pour the juice from the bowl into a 16-oz. glass or mason jar.

Drink on an empty stomach to get the most benefits.

BENEFITS

Soothes nerves	Promotes healthy skin	Supports healthy bones
Increases energy	High in vitamins C and B	Supports liver and kidney health
Anti-inflammatory		
Boost immune system		

CROWN CHAKRA FOODS

There are foods that support the stimulation and activation of the crown chakra, but the best sources of nourishment for this center are water, breath/prana, and sunshine. Being the highest center of spiritual awareness, the crown chakra is where we transcend body consciousness, and all thought matter, and rest completely in the awareness of Spirit. Solid foods, and foods in general, pull the consciousness down into the lower centers and cause us to dwell on the world of matter, thus disallowing the activation of the crown chakra. A half-day's fast or just a few hours of water, sunshine, and breathing exercises only will help open and balance the crown chakra and recharge it with fresh cosmic energy.

In essence, all food (and matter) is prana or life energy, but in a more materialized state. After consuming food, the body then has to break down the food that we eat and convert it into pure prana and energy for sustenance and vitality. We have little idea how much work we put our body's digestive system through, day in and day out, with our sometimes over abusive eating habits. It is not food alone that sustains our existence.

If you feed a seemingly dead body fruits and vegetables, it will fail to awaken with life. If you put the same body out in the sunshine and pump water into it, it will still be inanimate. Prana or life energy is the force that sustains life. Prana is the food of gods. Those who feast on this source of divine energy and life are granted the power to awaken from material consciousness and ascend higher in spiritual awareness.

Fasting has been a practice of spiritual adepts, yogis, and seekers since time immemorial and has been proven to improve mental and physical health. But before you attempt any fasts, please consult a professional doctor or nutritionist to ensure your safety.

Fasting offers the best rest to the body and brings remembrance of the soul.

CROWN CHAKRA AFFIRMATIONS

I accept myself as I am.

I am enough as I am.

I believe in myself.

I encourage myself.

I am worthy of all that my heart desires.

I am worthy of all that I dream.

I am a proud lover.

I am a proud dreamer.

I find joy in dreaming.

I find joy in loving.

I embrace all parts of my being.

It's okay to be myself.

I have something great to offer to the world.

My offering is love. My offering is myself.

I am needed.

I am valued.

I am appreciated.

I am Divine royalty.

I am cosmic nobility.

I am spiritually connected with all.

This connection allows me to be myself.

I am whole. I am wholeness.

I am complete as I am.

My soul is full of boundless joy.

My being is made of cosmic bliss.

I am the universe in ecstatic motion.

I live to be happy. I am happiness.

I share my happiness with all.

I accept the happiness of others as my own.

Life is full of abundance, beauty, and love.

I share my happiness with all.

I accept the happiness of others as my own.

My life is full of abundance, beauty, and love.

I am full of abundance, beauty, and love.

I attract high vibrational relationships.

I vibrate high vibrational love.

As my love expands, so does my awareness.

I am transcending fear.

I am transcending doubt.

I am transcending pride.

I am rising in courage.

I am rising in trust.

I am rising in service.

I am spiritually strong.

I am spiritually confident.

I am spiritually connected.

I am unattached and spiritually free.

I allow nothing to bind me.

I allow nothing to enslave me.

I allow nothing to control me.

I allow nothing to break me.

I am free. I am at peace.

I believe in the success of the world.

I contribute to the success of the world.

All people are my people.

All nations are my family.

My love is omnipresent.

My love is all-encompassing.

I am all-embracing.

I am all-pervading.

I am in everything.

Everything is within me.

POINTS OF DAILY INTROSPECTION

At the start of each day, the spiritual aspirant makes it a habit to practice impartial introspection. While viewing themselves with the soul's love and wisdom, inquire as to things that limit and suppress the expression of their highest nature. The following is a short list of introspective prompts that you may reflect upon during your morning meditation or journaling sessions.

- Am I afraid to be myself? If so, why?

- How frequently do I compare my life to others?

- How have the opinions of others shaped my personality?

- What environments make me feel *comfortable* with myself?

- What environments make me feel *uncomfortable* with myself?

- If I could spend a day alone anywhere in the world, where would I go?

- What books would I bring to keep me company?

- What is my idea of a perfect day?

POINTS OF NIGHTLY INTROSPECTION

At the end of each day, the spiritual aspirant makes it a habit to impartially introspect on that day's activities. Nightly introspection allows one to see whether they made spiritual progress and remained committed to the tasks, goals, and intentions established at the start of the day. Writing these things in a spiritual diary allows us to clearly see our repetitive faults and our virtues and make adjustments wherever needed. The following is a short list of introspective prompts that you may reflect upon during or after your nightly meditation.

- How much rest did I get today?

- When was the last time I took a day off?

- How did it feel to do absolutely nothing?

- How can I introduce rest into parts of my day?

- What am I chasing? And why am I chasing it?

- What can I empty myself of at this moment?

- How can I remind myself to be empty?

BEING YOURSELF
CAN ALSO LOOK LIKE:

Laughing

Creating

Dancing

Being playful

Traveling

Acting

Public speaking

Taking time to rest

Spending time alone

Doing what you love

Sharing your gifts

Allowing others to love you

Expressing how you feel

Sharing your thoughts

Appreciating who you are

Showing kindness to others

Forgiving your past

Allowing yourself to grow

Celebrating your uniqueness

When you really search for love
you will find it everywhere.

CHAKRA TONING

Those who understand the power of vibration hold in their hands a master key of healing and self-awakening. Chakra toning is an ancient technique that uses vowel sounds to balance each chakra. Vowels carry the "information energy" of speech, whereas consonants act to break up the energy flow. In ancient Indian, Chinese, and Kemetic cultures, vowel sounds are considered sacred as they yield tremendous physical and metaphysical benefits. You can use chakra toning as a simple, everyday technique to recalibrate the chakras and raise your vibration.

HOW TO PRACTICE:

Start by bringing yourself to a comfortable seated position. Inhale deeply, and as you exhale, bring your attention to the base of the spine. Inhale once more, and this time as you exhale, vocalize the vowel sound that corresponds to the root chakra. After doing so, pause briefly and continue to work up the spine, first inhaling, then exhaling as you vocalize the sound of each chakra.

- Root chakra vowel sound - "UUH," as in "cup."

- Sacral chakra vowel sound - "OOO," as in "you."

- Solar plexus vowel sound - "OH," as in "go."

- Heart chakra vowel sound - "AH," as in "father."

- Throat chakra vowel sound - "EYE," as in "my."

- Brow chakra vowel sound - "AYE," as in "say."

- Crown chakra vowel sound - "EEE" sound, as in "me."

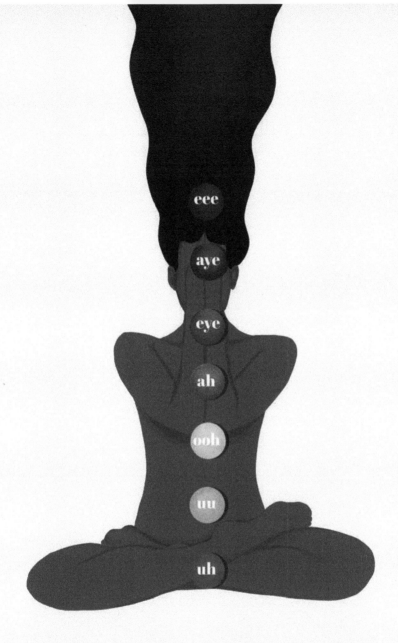

TIP: Remember to breathe out each sound as you ascend up the spine and through the chakras. Also, remember to pause briefly before going on to the next energy center. After practice, sit quietly for a few minutes and allow the vibrations to saturate your consciousness. You may also use this technique to focus solely on balancing one particular chakra if you want.

HEALING WITH
THE ELEMENTS

The elements of earth, water, fire, air, and ether (space) are fundamental life components. They are present not only in nature, but the elements are also a part of our physical nature. Neither the universe nor our physical existence would be possible if it were not for the presence of these essential energies. Every day we come in contact with and use each element's power, but we often unknowingly do not realize their value. If we seek to heal and harmonize our lives, it would be most beneficial to us to incorporate into our self-care routines exercises and practices that allow us to work with the elements consciously. Below are a few exercises and things you can do to work with each of the elements' energy. Feel free to explore and create your own ways of connecting and communing with elements. Make them fun and enjoyable to you!

HEALING WITH EARTH:

- Gardening, planting trees, plants, food, or simply playing in the soil and getting your hands dirty

- Hiking a trail or rock climbing

- Earthing (walking barefoot in grass, dirt, soil, or rocks)

- Bringing more plants into your home or living space

- Eating earth-grown foods or fasting

- Placing crystals on your body

- Physical exercises (Walking, running, yoga, tai chi, etc.)

- Climbing or hugging a tree

- Touching or laying down on the earth.

- Going on road trips or traveling abroad.

HEALING WITH WATER:

- Soaking in the bathtub

- Going for a swim

- Drinking fresh and high-quality water.

- Bringing movement to the hips

- Juice or water fasting

- Going boating or surfing

- Listening to the sounds of the ocean, waterfall, or river

- Speaking affirmations into the water you drink

- Doing Watsu (water massage)

- Dancing, walking, or playing in the rain

- Going to a water park

- Playing outdoor games that include the use of water

HEALING WITH FIRE:

- Burning sage, candles, or palo santo wood
- Fire gazing or sungazing
- Steaming or going to a sauna
- Yajna ceremony
- Agnihotra

HEALING WITH AIR:

- Doing pranayama
- Practicing breathing exercises
- Letting fresh air into your home or room

HEALING WITH ETHER (SPACE)

- Meditating
- Sound healing
- Singing
- Having healthy conversations.
- Fasting
- Chanting mantras
- Listening to healing music.

How you heal is totally up to you.

NOTES

NOTES

NOTES

_____

_____

_____

_____

_____

_____

_____

_____

_____

_____

_____

_____

_____

_____

_____

_____

NOTES

NOTES

NOTES

NOTES

SELF-CARE PACKAGE: HEALING THROUGH THE CHAKRAS

NOTES

NOTES

NOTES

NOTES

NOTES

NOTES

NOTES

NOTES

NOTES

NOTES

NOTES

NOTES

NOTES

Lightning Source UK Ltd.
Milton Keynes UK
UKHW021242140821
388628UK00005BA/192/J